MW00322898

But Mary Kept All These Things

Advent Devotions
Rooted in the Christmas Gospel

W. S. Carter

CSS Publishing Company, Inc
Lima, Ohio

FIRST EDITION
Copyright © 2021
by CSS Publishing Co., Inc.

Published by CSS Publishing Company, Inc., Lima, Ohio 45807. All rights reserved. No part of this publication may be reproduced in any manner whatsoever without the prior permission of the publisher, except in the case of brief quotations embodied in critical articles and reviews. Inquiries should be addressed to: CSS Publishing Company, Inc., Permissions Department, 5450 N. Dixie Highway, Lima, Ohio 45807.

Scripture quotations marked (RSV) are from the Revised Standard Version of the Bible, copyrighted 1946, 1952 ©, 1971, 1973, by the Division of Christian Education of the National Council of the Churches of Christ in the USA. Used by permission.

Library of Congress Cataloging-in-Publication Data :

Names: Carter, W. S. (William S.), 1946- author. Title: But Mary kept all these things : Advent devotions rooted in the Christmas Gospel / W.S. Carter. Description: First edition. | Lima, Ohio : CSS Publishing Company, Inc., [2020] Identifiers: LCCN 2020036915 | ISBN 9780788030147 (paperback) | ISBN 9780788030154 (ebook) Subjects: LCSH: Mary, Blessed Virgin, Saint--Prayers and devotions. | Advent--Prayers and devotions. | Christmas--Prayers and devotions. Classification: LCC BT608.5 .C37 2020 | DDC 242/.332--dc23 LC record available at https://lccn.loc.gov/2020036915

For more information about CSS Publishing Company resources, visit our website at www.csspub.com, email us at csr@csspub.com, or call (800) 241-4056.

e-book:
ISBN-13: 978-0-7880-3015-4
ISBN-10: 0-7880- 3015-9

ISBN-13: 978-0-7880-3100-7
ISBN-10: 0-7880-3014-0

ELECTRONICALLY PRINTED

For Petra Lily

"Sharing our stories reminds us of what we believe in and helps us make sense of a fickle world. They are common, yet we tell them because our experiences are so uncommon. No two stories are ever the same, even when told by the same person, using the same words."

Colum McCaan

"The third shepherd… 'What is real
about us all is that each of us is waiting.'"

From *For the Time Being* by W. H. Auden

"How good it is that you can be at home to celebrate Advent."
From *Letters and Papers From Prison* by Dietrich Bonhoeffer

Contents

Preparing The Way Of The Lord

Luke 3:1-6: *In the fifteenth year of the reign of Emperor Tiberius, when Pontius Pilate was governor of Judea, and Herod was ruler of Galilee, and his brother Philip ruler of the region of Iturea and Trachonitis, and Lysander ruler of Abilene, during the high priesthood of Annas and Caiaphas, the Word of God came to John son of Zechariah in the wilderness. He went into all the region around the Jordan, proclaiming a baptism of repentance for the forgiveness of sins, as it is written in the book of the words of the prophet Isaiah, "The voice of one crying out in the wilderness: 'Prepare the way of the Lord, make his paths straight. Every valley shall be filled, and every mountain and hill shall be made low, and the crooked shall be made straight, and the rough ways made smooth; and all flesh shall see the salvation of God.'"*

Just after Thanksgiving a few years ago we went on our church's NYC Bus Trip and went on our own to the Metropolitan Museum of Art on Fifth Avenue to see their majestic Christmas tree. We do it every year. When it is all decorated, it has eighteenth century terracotta Neapolitan Angels flying in the boughs and an amazing village scene surrounding the crèche, all the way around the base of the entire tree, including shepherds and wise men, a camel, a horse, and an elephant! There are sheep of course, but also a baker, a goat herd, someone fishing on the bank of a stream, even a minstrel with bagpipes!

It is an amazing, classic, New York holiday destination. As we were there in late November, it was still "under construction," with volunteers and museum workers climbing ladders and setting the angels in the branches, and others on their knees working on the beautiful scene, placing the myriad of beautiful figures underneath the lower branches. In the center are Mary and Joseph and, of course in a manger, Jesus, in a perfectly picturesque stable; all placed amid the ruins of Roman columns and statuary — because the eighteenth century artists in Naples knew that Christ came to Bethlehem, but Christ also came, they knew, to their own environs in their own time. That made it Christmas. May it be so for you and yours this year. Christmas is sometimes one of those things that seems to start before it actually begins. But when it arrives, it arrives where you are.

That year, early as we were, Advent had just begun, of course. The huge Christmas tree and scene beneath it was still being prepared, not yet complete. Screens blocked our view. Though there were some gaps through which you could catch glimpses of a score of workers. Around back, in the rear, there was a quiet, almost secret opening, and we spent long minutes watching an elegantly tall and poised woman. She was ever so patiently and lovingly, unpacking figures from a huge, stenciled museum storage crate, gently dusting them one by one with a small, soft, paint brush. She was so attentive to what she was doing that it was absolutely transfixing to watch her.

In the years since, during Advent, I often remember that scene, especially that woman. I also sometimes imagine, in my mind's eye, that I can see my grown son, Ryan, unpacking his family's Christmas tree in their porch room, miles away, unfolding the branches with the lights already on them, Petra watching attentively, perhaps standing on tip-toe to hang one of her (fragile!) ornaments herself.

It is wonderful to watch someone "prepare the way of the Lord", as Luke said it. It can be especially moving to watch quietly, almost secretly... gently, from a distance. The preparation you do each Advent is also a treasure to be cherished for itself as Christmas nears. You are preparing your hearts, as the decorations are placed in your house and outside, as you seek a tree and get it home. The baking, shopping, and wrapping, even reading the pages in a book.... These things are all Advent treasures to cherish, not just a to-do list with a deadline.

When this Christmas finally arrives, may you recall all these Advent preparations, and may all the preparing you have watched done, so carefully and lovingly by others over the years, inspire you in the days ahead. May all who gather with you, even in your mind's eye, be lovingly present to share great joy at the birth of Christ. May Jesus be born, right on time, and fill your heart with the joy of his presence, even as you prepare. May you and yours come to know the presence of God that can feel simply abundant, even when you may have expected something perhaps a little less; both when the stable occupies the perfect place, and even when the old columns seem to crumble around the edges.

In these shortening days of Advent, may you know the light that radiates hope and joy and wholeness and reveals to all flesh, "the salvation of God."

But Mary Kept All These Things

Ever faithful God, your prophets foretold the coming of the light. We confidently, and with patience, await the coming of your son and the day when he will gather all people to live in your light. Amen.

Ponder These Things

Luke 2:19: But Mary kept all these things, pondering them in her heart.

Every Advent, my thoughts run ahead to the Nativity; the birth and the manger. I can't help it. That scene is the center. Absolutely everything else is trimming, garnish, a setting of beauty indeed; but the stone, the gem, the pearl of great price will be laid before us freely in the simple story of the manger and the figures gathered there as the darkness falls. The Word made flesh — the incarnation.

The preparation for that good news through our Advent musings can show us not just the charm of Christmas, but proclaim to us good news that can provide safety, strength, and healing all year long.

The whole story expands slowly from the center. We remember that Gabriel told Mary, and months later, the angels told the shepherds, and they told those at the manger what had happened to them on the hillside, while they were tending to the sheep. The shepherds, delivering this message, left and went off "glorifying God" for all they had experienced, "all they had heard and seen…" They were thrilled to be a part of the story, and yet amazingly, they seemed to march right out of the story…. They vanished from the scene, from the gospels, even from legends.

I can't speak for you, but I'd rather not march right out of the story. That's one of the things I ponder each Advent. Mary pondered too. (This story Luke told is the place I learned to enjoy the word and the process of pondering.) She is the only adult in the story who continued into Jesus' ministry; not Joseph, not the shepherds, not an innkeeper or a midwife — only Mary… the ponderer.

In Advent, we often think of Mary's response at the annunciation, when the Archangel Gabriel came to her in Nazareth to tell her she would bear a child. I also think our minds run ahead to the manger at the center. I think it can be a good thing to ponder the reality of Christmas story in Advent — the gemstone, the child in the manger. Is Advent our own version of the annunciation?

But Mary Kept All These Things

Turn it over in your mind. Ponder that question in your heart, put it in your pocket. Fondle it, draw it out in the light of the first Advent candle.... Look at it. Take it out of the pocket in your heart when you are at work or in class this month. Advent means "coming" of course, but Advent just as often means "anticipation" to me.

A gift is being prepared for you, a Savior for you. A healing, a strengthening in the broken places; a quiet confidence in a Savior. That is the gift being prepared for you.

Perhaps you don't feel the need of a Savior this Advent. Perhaps your credit cards are not maxed out yet, perhaps the wrapping is already finished, or just maybe the reality of Advent has enfolded you with sense of quiet and expectant joy, and you are simply well. That is wonderful. Perhaps you don't feel the need of the gift right yet.

You have some idea though, of what's coming, don't you? Ponder that. God works this Advent season, before Christmas comes, and even afterwards!

Don't forget, Mary was still pondering when Jesus stayed behind in the temple when he was twelve years old, and said he was just about his Father's business (remember, he was in the temple, yet Joseph ran a carpenter's shop...). She was still pondering when she told Jesus they were short of wine at the wedding in Cana. She was still pondering when he said to a crowd that his mother and his brothers were those who did God's will. Still pondering I believe, even when tears streaked her face on the day of his crucifixion.

The time may very well come when you will feel in need of the gift of a Savior. And the story at the center of that, the story of Christmas, is coming soon. It is a beautiful story. Here's wishing you a beautiful Advent waiting for it to come true again and come to you once more, this year. Happy pondering.

Come Jesus, enter our lives this Advent. We hear many voices encouraging us to prepare for your arrival. We are confident that the time is right, for you have chosen it; through Jesus Christ, your Son, our Lord who lives and rules with you and the Holy Spirit, one God, within our world today. Amen.

Be Prepared To Stop

Luke 2:11: *For to you is born this day in the city of David, a Savior, who is Christ the Lord.*

When we are alert or moving into new territory, we notice signs. There are signs of Advent's progress that we expect and know: Advent Wreaths, evergreen trees tied to the tops of automobiles, Christmas lights outlining houses or candles in windows, even carols can be part of the countdown.

We know traffic signs better, we see them all year round: Yield, Stop, Merge Left, One Lane Road Ahead, etc. Recently I was confronted by a sign that was new to me — *Be Prepared To Stop,* it commanded! Probably repairs on the small bridge, I thought as I drove along a rural road in Litchfield County, Connecticut. This road is one I drive infrequently frankly, only when looking for some peace. I always think of it as the road from here to there. The road from here to there and back again of course.

On our Advent road to Bethlehem and back, did you notice there is almost always a return in the story? But we are getting ahead of ourselves.

"Be prepared to stop, " the sign said. It was only on my way home that I realized the sign was posed on both sides of the road. Be prepared to stop, in both directions, both going to and coming from Christmas. How do we come to know that? We read the gospel stories; Angels told the shepherds, remember, just as Luke said. Remember?

In the first scene, Jesus was born, almost quietly; "the time came for her to be delivered... gave birth... wrapped... laid in a manger." Blink then, and shift then to the second scene. The shepherds on their hillside were settling down for the peace of a quiet night watching their flocks. They were sleeping rough, as befits their profession and their reputation; rough and ready, able to adapt and overcome and make do. They were outlaws of sorts in first-century Palestine in fact. A bit of tarnish on them, kind of like us it seems to me. I'm not sure they were prepared to stop, but they certainly did stop what they were doing that night and a bit tarnished or not, they became the center of attention.

"Christ is born," they were told. And yet, in the midst of the angelic announcement, the focus was on the shepherds: The focus was on them, and I believe as we move through Advent, the focus is on us, the heirs of those who are slightly less than perfect shepherds who heard the news, stopped doing what they were in the middle of, and made their way down the hill to Bethlehem. Then came back again. The angels would announce the birth of a Savior (to you, to us, to them) and in that moment, as earth is touched by heaven, a connection will be made again in our time just as surely as it was then.

The shepherds went to the stable to see the sign they had been told to look for. Not one candle had been lit on their Advent wreath, they had not seen one sign that warned them to be prepared to stop. Yet as the angels sang, heaven touched them. The shepherds were halted by angels, the wise men were led by a star. How have you have been led onto this Advent path? By the signs, the images, the phrases, the memories, the proclamation, and the songs of faith that have been signs for generations.

Even in the marketing mayhem of modern shopping malls, every now and then you can hear a Christmas carol that goes beyond winter weather or Frosty's "corncob pipe, and two eyes made out of coal...". Every now and then you can hear a carol that names the sacred reality of God coming to earth. Be prepared to stop then, just for a moment.

You will be the center of attention as your personal Advent moment melts ever so slowly into Christmas. You, like the shepherds, will be the center of God's attention. The message is for you. That is the truth of the gospel, that is the good news. "For to you is born... in the city of David, a Savior which is Christ the Lord." City, Savior, David, Lord — but you are the center of attention, whether you were really prepared to stop or not; you go along chasing after that moment, there and back again, already knowing, almost remembering the angels' song, sung in years past, word for word.

Are you still looking for a sign? Look around you, but be prepared to stop when you notice it — let it enter your through eyes, into your ears, your heart... be prepared to stop, you are the center of attention. Like the shepherds, the first ones told, be prepared to stop — prepare to celebrate, even for a secret moment, the fact of our faith that a Savior is coming into the world.

We are ready to believe it, even if not exactly ready yet to be exactly sure. But it is true. Be prepared to stop on the road there, and the road back. Remember, that's a command, not a question. Remember — don't ever forget.

The road through Advent to Christmas has always been about you, and about your return to your home place; saved, redeemed, and at the center of God's attention. Advent marks, day by day, the return of God into your life. Be prepared to stop!

Dear God, alert us to the reality of your coming. Sharpen our senses and fill us with watchful expectation. Help us to be ready to stop. Help us to share our joy, through the glory of what God is doing. Amen.

An Advent Cappuccino

Luke 2:12 *"And this will be a sign for you: you will find a babe wrapped in swaddling clothes and lying in a manger."*

Advent or not, my primary image is of the manger. It is God's sign: "This will be a sign for you, you will find a babe, wrapped in swaddling clothes, and lying in a manger..."

A child was born in a cave to save the world. A child was born in a stable to save the world. A child was laid in a manger to save the world. A child was laid on the straw to save the world.

Someone has suggested that, to the child, all this seemed enormous — his mother's hand, her breast, the steam from the ox's nostrils, Joseph's beard, his glowing lantern, even the sorrows and losses and evils of the world. (Could he possibly have known that Herod's soldiers would soon be on the way?)

Everything he saw was enormous. From his vantage point, the Christmas tree in your home is gigantic. Your worries loom large. The child in the straw sees them, more enormous though they may be, and comprehends them; even in this time we call Advent.

What do you see? I bet you see just a child in a manger, in your mind's eye; in a cave, in a stable, in a manger, in the straw. It may not be what you would like to see. My granddaughter, Petra, when she was four, took him out of the manger we have lined with real straw. She took him away from the animals and wrapped the baby in one of her doll's blankets. Then she put Mary nearby to care for him. That was Petra being kind, as she still is, and caring. She wanted to take care of the Son of God.

But this baby came to be in the straw. He came to see and to bear the enormous pains, losses, sorrows, and worries of our world. He came to comprehend them and to draw them to himself.

The child reached out... even in Advent in my considered opinion. We can see images from artistic renderings across many centuries... the child reaching out to tug on his mother's veil, her face or cheek,

17

reaching for Joseph's beard or his lantern, or to touch the cloud of steam from the animals' breath.

The image is everywhere, "*Il segno*" they say in Italy, "the sign". The image of the sign, "You will find a babe…" is everywhere. Sometimes it is on the first Christmas cards to arrive at your home; it is on the postcards decorating my study this Advent, even on the walls of the most prestigious museums 365 days a year. Sometimes you see the baby naked, sometimes you can see the straw, and sometimes a beautiful blanket is protecting the child. I recently pondered an enormous painting of the nativity by a Netherlandish master of the early sixteenth century by the name of Jan Gossart. He rendered a gothic roof of it all, to draw you in. It drew me in, for my Advent contemplation that afternoon in the museum.

In psychiatry there is a concept called the capuchin complex. It is good to think about it in Advent, it seems to me. It means to pull a hood over one's self. It means to sit down, hunched over, underneath something – like a Capuchin monk sheltered by his hood… concentrating. In Advent, psychiatry aside, in our best moments we concentrate. We hope to find time to contemplate. Perhaps over an Advent cappuccino, named for the color of the Capuchin monks' robes. We concentrate on Joseph, on Mary, on their journey to Bethlehem. We sift through our knowledge and trust in the sign of the coming of the child in the manger.

I like the hood. I like the concentration of everything focusing in and in on one image — which is what you have in the sign of the manger scene; in a cave, in a stable, in the manger, in the straw, under a sheltering gigantic gothic roof thanks to an artist I'd never heard of until that Advent afternoon. Though the picture has hung there for years saying, "Come in for a while, under this shelter."

You might think there is a centrifugal force pressing the news out from the cave, out from the manger, out to the shepherds, to the wise men, to the world. It is after all the Christmas story that we are anticipating this Advent; waiting to hear, though we know it by heart, the proclamation of the angels to the shepherds, the proclamation of the salvation of the world: "For to you is born this day in the city of David a Savior which is Christ the Lord!" You would be right of course. You might even sing "Go Tell It On The Mountain" on Christmas. It is something like tossing a rock or a pebble in a pond. Out and out and out the ripples will go, telling the story. The radius keeps widening out from the central figure of the child.

But, especially in Advent, in essence, it is exactly the other way around. In the facts of our faith, it is quite the opposite in Advent. In Advent, the force is first and foremost centripetal; it draws us to the center. The manger is almost magnetic; it draws us toward the child, into the stable, under the hood.

Sometimes in the paintings, the baby tugs on his mother's scarf or veil and looks at her. Sometimes the artist allows his eyes to look directly at us and draw us.... Into the cave, into the stable, into the straw, under the gigantic gothic roof to remind you that he comes to comprehend your most enormous sorrow, to celebrate your most enormous joy and to remind you of the cross as well as the power of the resurrection in your life, and in mine. Who would be helped by such a reminder? Yes, in Advent?

At the foundation of all the anticipation and expectation of Advent is God's sacrificial love and the pure love seen in the joy of the nativity. "God so loved the world, that he sent his only begotten Son..." There, where everything started, is where everything really begins. In God's love, and in news about joy. It is Advent, the joy of his coming is drawing closer each day. Coming to the stable, to the straw in the manger. Under the roof. Under the hood. In joy. In your concentrated gaze. Drawing us in, closer.

I know, we have been anticipating and celebrating for 20 centuries. When we celebrate the day of his birth this year, he'll be 2,020 or so. Today is Wednesday, tomorrow will be Thursday. How mundane. It is an anniversary that we get to observe him without adding one wrinkle to his face..., how astounding. How unimportant.

Here's the deal: In this dark, cold season a child will be born in a manger, and will be born again in our hearts to save the world. But always try to remember that the force is centripetal in Advent. It is drawing us nearer and nearer. A child will be born in a manger to save those you love. A child will be born in a manger to save you. It seems only reasonable and extraordinarily faithful to begin to feel God's love for you this Advent, to trust the signs, and prepare for the joy!

Holy Father, Christ is coming. Our King. Our Savior. Our hearts are filling with joy day by day this Advent. May we not be too busy or too happy to quietly bow our heads and hearts, and concentrate; help us to slowly and gently contemplate the centripetal force your Spirit is exerting on our world. We pray in the name of the one who is coming, Jesus Christ, your Son, our Lord. Amen.

Almost...

Luke 2:8-9 *"In that region there were shepherds living in the fields, keeping watch over their flock by night. Then an angel of the Lord stood before them, and the glory of the Lord shone around them, and they were terrified."*

Do you have a scene beneath your Christmas tree? Some thirty years ago, when we served a church in Fairfield Connecticut, friends there had a city under their tree. I hadn't seen one in a long, long time. There were fifty plastic houses, fire trucks, skaters, the whole Megillah. Otto set up the tree, decorated it, and put the cityscape under it all on Christmas Eve, so they always came to the late service. His wife Mary was always afraid they would be late, she told me.

When I was a child, my Dad chose our tree and lugged it home (sometimes I got to help) from the local tree stand, about five blocks away from our apartment. Then, under my Mother's critical eye, we put it in a stand and turned it round and round to get the best side showing; sometimes Dad would cut a branch off, drill a hole in a new place on the trunk and put it in, or with twine, tie one or two sagging branches up to more vigilant poses. Then came the lights, ornaments, and finally, tinsel.

But the scene underneath the tree was solo Mom work. It was a labor of love really. A white sheet represented the snowy fields of Bethlehem... no city, no skaters, no fire trucks. Just a stable, Mary, Joseph, an ox, a donkey, manger with a child in it. Then, off to the right, around the tree there was a hill. It was a real project, lying on the cold linoleum floor, the lowest branches framing her head as she made the hill from a paper bag and smoothed the sheet over it. The sheep had one solid base each. The angel of the Lord, likewise, had an oval base for firm footing. But the two shepherds stood on their small feet. I remember that getting them to stand up on the sheet with the crumpled bag underneath was a project of patience. Mom was afraid they would fall over if she didn't place them perfectly. But they did, on more than one occasion.

The angel and the shepherds were with their flock on their hillside with a crumpled paper bag beneath — almost a bit unstable. Imagine the darkness of the world that night, only some stars, perhaps a moon, perhaps not. Perhaps there was a campfire and then the shepherds were surprised by heaven's glory, and struck with fear: the glory of the Lord!

What might that even mean, "The glory of the Lord?" I like to think that if you were an infant or a well-loved six-year-old enfolded in your grandfather's arms, you would laugh when the glory of the Lord broke upon you. One of those gentle echoes of delight that seem, however loud or soft, to start in their toes and resonate down deep in their tummy and vocalize out of their open mouth! The glory of the Lord must be almost like that for the innocent children of God's kingdom.

But for adults, like many of us, the glory of the Lord is almost good, almost not so good, like the shepherds. Almost on the edge of polite, almost not smart enough while also being almost too smart for their own good, similar to me, and you too, I suspect.

We are at first afraid of the glory of the Lord, even the shepherds "they were terrified," or as Luke said: "filled with fear" in the translation of my growing up. All of us shepherd types are at first afraid, and the angel, God's messenger, had to speak. How long before the angel of the Lord spoke? A second? Or forty seconds, or was it almost an hour of uncertainty? The angel was hovering, the shepherds were fearful. How long have you been waiting to set a certain uncertainty or fear aside this Advent?

Don't be afraid. (You knew the angel would say that didn't you?) But listen... "*I bring you good news of a great joy that is for all the people...*" I hope that you are almost not afraid. I hope you are almost in awe this Advent. I hope you are back on your two feet, a little unsteady, but up, on the top of the hill underneath that Christmas tree, waiting for what will come next.

Let's take a lingering look at this almost-Advent scene on the hill over Bethlehem, beneath a Christmas tree, announcing Christ's coming. The shepherds, having listened to the message of salvation, are almost understanding, almost letting go of their fear, trying to believe, standing on their two shaky legs, with their mouths almost agape... It's almost the most appropriate Advent pose.

Even with only one candle lit this first week of Advent, we almost understand, beyond our personal fears and uncertainties, that there will soon be a child lying in the manger, swaddled, wrapped in bands of cloth, so well-loved, even in a stable. King Solomon was swaddled as a child, the Bible tells us, it was a sign of being loved. God's love is almost incomprehensible, isn't it? *"God so loved the world…"* From the wood of the manger to the wood of the cross, salvation's journey is from birth to death to new life. We may need almost all of Advent to take it in.

It was, I believe now, all of Advent there in that scene beneath our Christmas tree in my childhood home. The stable was front and center, with the holy family, and just around the corner to the right, underneath the branches, the precariously upright (most of the time) shepherds. On the white sheet, on the level, and on the hill, they never got together. It was an Advent scene of expectation, of anticipation, of promise.

It was the moment just before the story comes alive. It was and is an Advent scene, as we wait, almost managing our fears and uncertainties. You are important to the babe lying in the manger, just as you are. You are almost good — almost not so good — just as you are. Truly, his coming birth is a sign for you. I'm almost sure you will find him, but if not, you can trust him to find you.

Dear Father, we live in the midst of an uncertain, risk-filled world. But even here we can be secure within your care. Help us to listen to the promptings of your Spirit, and to trust in your love; through Jesus Christ, your Son our Lord, who lives and rules with you and the Holy Spirit, one God, within our world today. Amen.

Paper Bag Hill

Luke 2:15. *"When the angels went away from them into heaven, the shepherds said to one another, "Let us go over to Bethlehem and see this thing that has happened, which the Lord has made known to us."*

Throughout Advent, each and every one of us are invited to make a journey toward the light, toward the center of the story, toward the manger.

Through the four Sundays of Advent in my previous church, we had a simple manger, filled with straw. The manger, each week, was moved down the aisle; from its start in the rear of the sanctuary, closer and closer to the altar each week. It was brought closer each week to center stage. Really though, if we think about it, it is the manger that attracts us to move closer and closer to it.

As Luke told the story, there is action across the fields on a dark night, perhaps under a moon. When I was a child, as I've told you, under our Christmas tree my mother would set up the family manger scene on a white sheet with the stable, the holy family, and the animals. Then, on a hillside made of a paper bag crumpled up under the white sheet, she placed the shepherds, watching their flocks by night, and the angel, the messenger of God.

That is precisely how Luke set the scene too. That is how it began. The angels appeared and announced the good news of a Savior... *"and the shepherds said to one another, 'Let us go over to Bethlehem and see this thing that has happened, which the Lord has made known to us.'"* To them and to us. We are making our way too, this Advent, drawn as they were by the sign of the manger. Everyone on the hillside comes to the stable, drawn by the light, by the warmth, by the message, the age old message of God's love.

Shepherds, just to notice one of the details that Luke gave us, have been made sort of romantic and somewhat noble down through the centuries. They have taken on the gentleness of their flocks, but they were neither gentle nor noble. They were rough and ready. Their reputation was for an occasional dishonesty, sometimes just a bit outside the law. Sinners, I guess, like me and you, not to be too presumptuous.

As a boy, I always appreciated the care my mother lavished on the arrangement of the shepherds and their sheep on that paper bag hill. Camping out there, under the moon, (there had to be a moon)... that was my favorite place in the story, even before I came to know it was where Luke the evangelist, the good news storyteller, wanted me to find myself.

The shepherds came to the manger, and when they saw the announced sign fulfilled, they went back to their camp, back to their home, on Paper Bag Hill, glorifying and praising God for all they had heard and seen, and they went on with their lives.

As you close this book today and go off to decorate your home or wrap some gifts on Paper Bag Hill, Paper Chase, Lenora Drive, Broadway, or wherever you live, notice all through your Advent, preparing for the celebration, that you too are glorifying and praising God in all your preparations. Isn't that what Advent is about after all? Yes, glorifying and praising God in all our preparations.

The angels sang to the shepherds under the moon on Paper Bag Hill about what God had done, what God was doing. The manger, shepherds, even the angels were all serving the story of what God had done, so you and I and our children's children can come to know the faith that gives us energy as we prepare, even as we live in the hope and the joy of what God has done, what God is doing.

God was sending his son, born of a woman, to live in our midst. He was sending him to suffer, to die, to rise again, to enter the story of our lives, to grow up with us, to struggle with us, and to celebrate with us. He sent him to go on with our lives with us, to save us, to keep company with us through the ultimate dangers of this life, and to make real the promise of the life to come.

May this Advent prepare us all to remember his manger. It is the foundational safe space, the beginning of salvation. It is the beginning. But what a beginning! We are off to a fine beginning, aren't we?

O Lord, you are coming! May we prepare well for your arrival! Teach us to trust your word and to celebrate your coming among us. Fill us with joy through Jesus Christ, your son, our Lord, this day and every day. Amen.

Do Not Push

Matthew 1:18-19 *"Now the birth of Jesus the Messiah took place in this way. When his mother Mary had been engaged to Joseph, but before they lived together, she was found to be with child from the Holy Spirit. Her husband Joseph, being a righteous man and unwilling to expose her to public disgrace, planned to dismiss her quietly."*

My favorite truck of Advent has always been the big brown truck of the United Parcel Service, what my Mother called "the UPS truck." I have nothing against FedEx or the rest, but in my childhood, it was the UPS truck that brought Christmas packages from Minnesota, from Pennsylvania, and from Long Island to my house, or actually, to 782 East 32nd Street in Brooklyn, New York, apartment A8. They had the address on the packages, no star needed for these contemporary wise men, bearing gifts in their brown UPS trucks. (No GPS either! God bless them...)

Driving around one recent Advent, looking for my Christmas sermon, I fell in behind an orange truck, not a brown one, an orange one. It was a State of Connecticut Department of Transportation truck. Often I am grateful in winter, as they spread sand ahead of me, or plow back one more swath of slush. I have followed more than one state truck ploddingly home, very gratefully during a winter storm. But this was a nice day, a dry road, and I was looking for an image for my sermon... I didn't expect this delay, much as Joseph didn't expect his challenge. I was driving up and down the roads, on chilly gentle hills complete with double lines, and I was impatient. (All the patience of Advent can drain out of preachers in the teens of December.) I was looking for an image.

There on the back of that dump truck, high up across the back panel, was a three word message — in big block letters — I was close enough to read it. It was painted on long ago, designed, I suppose, to help other state workers know how best to load the box of the truck. It simply said: *"Do Not Push."* Perhaps it was a message for Joseph. It was most certainly a message for me: *Do not push.* Don't push it. It will come.

But Mary Kept All These Things

Christmas will come. It is so very close. But not close enough to touch it — not yet. As close as I was to the rear of the truck, close enough to read the letters, but not close enough to touch it. *Do not push.* Back away from the manger for a moment or two. Consider Joseph and the possibility that it's a hard road in front of us too, one that may admit of very few easy answers.

Here we sit in the normal haste and worries of our pre-Christmas lives. We hear the carols on the car radio and see the decorations everywhere. Perhaps it is in this way, in this generation, that the invitation comes to us, or challenges us, eludes us, or annoys us. The truck helped me. I think if I were Joseph's rabbi or his friend, I would find a way to rephrase the sign; "*Do Not Push.*" Wait, just a little longer. Listen for just another moment or two, don't rush ahead, and don't pass these Advent moments by.

So, here we are. A bit like Joseph sometimes, faced with dark challenges that leave us yearning for some help, a bit like the shepherds in the days and hours before the heavenly host arrived. In the darkness and worries of our lives, in our worst moments we see only by the flickering, chancy campfires of our haunted hopefulness and fragile faithfulness in the daunting darkness of the twenty-first century.

Do not push. For tonight and tomorrow, for as long as you can hold on to the sight and sound of it, see the promise to Mary, Joseph's betrothed, who was with child. Do not push. Lay hold of the good news of the promise. The rest will come soon enough; you will not miss the reassurance of Joseph in his dream or the angel of the Lord's announcement as the flocks lie sleeping, the boy in Joseph's carpenter's shop, the teacher on the hillside, the Christ on the cross, or Mary Magdalene in the Garden. Advent is about all of God's promises.

But Advent is not, finally, all about us, stuck behind a truck, uncertain or aching about our current situation, straining to get somewhere, even somewhere important, faster. Advent is about God. Life is about God. Love is about God. Forgiveness is about God. Healing is about God.

For the days to come — *Do Not Push*. Anticipate gently. Do what you can to live a patient Advent life. Lighting two more candles, one candle at a time…

Come, Lord, we praise the way you enter our lives. Give us patience to receive your story with happiness and joy and expectation; through Jesus Christ, your Son, our Lord, who lives and rules with you and the Holy Spirit, one God, within our world today. Amen.

Carry A Tree To Bethlehem

Matthew 3:1-10 *"In those days John the Baptist appeared in the wilderness of Judea, proclaiming, "Repent, for the kingdom of heaven has come near." This is the one of whom the prophet Isaiah spoke when he said, "the voice of one crying out in the wilderness; Prepare the way of the Lord, make his paths straight." Now John wore clothing of camel's hair with a leather belt around his waist, and his food was locusts and wild honey. Then the people of Jerusalem and all Judea were going out to him, and all the region along the Jordan, and they were baptized by him in the river Jordan, confessing their sins. But when he saw so many Pharisees and Sadducees coming for baptism, he said to them, "You brood of vipers! Who warned you to flee from the wrath to come? Bear fruit worthy of repentance. Do not presume to say to yourselves, 'We have Abraham as our ancestor'; for I tell you, God is able from these stones to raise up children to Abraham. Even now the ax is lying at the root of the trees; every tree therefore that does not bear good fruit is cut down and thrown into the fire."*

Our tree usually comes home by this second week of Advent, the fruit of a cold walk around a New Hartford Christmas Tree farm in Connecticut. Most of our years there we have gone to the same place, we like to find one and cut it down. They wrap it up in that clear plastic netting and pull it through a bright red machine that looks for all the world like a hoop that lions and tigers would jump through at the Madison Square Garden Ringling Brothers Barnum and Bailey Circus' of my childhood. The netting makes it easier to transport on the roof of our car, and then get it through our door and into the house. It even stays on while the tree is anchored into the stand in our living room, which we had put in place before we left.

Advent preparation is like good cooking practice… get your *"mise en place"* ready as the first order of business. The kit for the tree hunt includes, not an "axe… at the root of the tree," rather, I use my veteran Swedish bow saw, an old sheet to protect the car's roof and some

27

clothesline rope for lashing it securely atop the car, as well as some veteran gloves that can get a little sappy. Thankfully, in these recent years, they have supplied a little metal-frame cart with bicycle wheels to get the tree easily from the place we find it growing and cut it down, to the place where we pay for it and watch the red machine do its work. We get a little help loading it on, and then drive home with our Christmas tree. It has been an Advent treasure and pleasure in our family for many years.

There is a legend of the sixteenth-century German reformer Martin Luther, trudging home through a forest one December night, and looking up through the branches and glimpsing the star-strewn sky over Wittenberg. They say he cut down a fir tree and brought it into the house, past his wife Katie's shocked expression, and went about putting candles on it so the lit tree would remind their children of "the night sky over Bethlehem that first Christmas."

Each year we have a tree. Each year we decorate it together, while John Denver and the muppets sing Christmas Carols. Each year we try to find one new ornament to add to the many others in the box that are treasures from the past and will always be on each tree. There are things that seem to be a perfect part of our tree; some always go on the bottom or the top, some are items of negotiation as they lend their beauty, their color, their remembered story, and thus, their gift, to our Advent preparations. Some remain in the box, perhaps to be part of next year's decorations. We have had taller trees, squatter ones, and ones that had to be turned to put their best face toward the room. We even remember "the year of the perfect tree."

From Avon by way of Wittenberg to Bethlehem, it may seem a strange route. But when you are moving your spirit toward home, through Advent toward Christmas, even the most circuitous route can be a good one. And sometimes, as Luther thought, it takes a tree. All of us are on our way home this Advent, to Bethlehem once more, if only the Bethlehem in our hearts.

The netting is helpful in getting the tree home, but once in the stand, it has outlived its usefulness. It doesn't look like a Christmas tree yet, it looks more like a big green tuna, hung dockside, so you can have your photo taken with it, out of water. With my sharp little knife, gently off with the netting, and there it stands — our Christmas tree.

Slowly, in a matter of hours, the branches settle down into the gentle arms-outstretched, uplifted, almost prayerful gesture that you picture in your mind as you are reading these words.

But Mary Kept All These Things

May you spend some of your waiting and preparing and anticipating time this Advent prayerfully, in the Bethlehem of your heart, the home place which God in Christ will visit this Christmas and every Christmas, as God in Christ has for ages. As you set your tree in its stand and hang your decorations, may you anticipate the fact of our faith that God is coming. Blue spruce or Scotch pine, Canadian balsam or Fraser fir, or one fresh from a box, topped by an angel or a star… Christ is coming. Hung with white lights or colored, steady or blinking — Christ is coming. Surrounded by gifts or a snow scene or electric trains… Christ is coming.

I hope this year no one in your family has a feeling of being pulled through some bright red machine themselves. I hope the essence of carols, cards, prayers, and candles will cut the netting, and let you and your family's lives be settled into yet another joyful faithful Advent, complete with the precise amount of brightness and ornamentation that makes Christmas true for you and yours. May you spend the rest of this Advent in the Bethlehem of your heart.

Come, Lord. We hear your messenger speaking words of judgment and of hope. Enter our lives and turn them around, from watching others to watching for you. Strengthen the roots of our faith and lift our hearts to you. We pray in the name of him who is coming, Jesus Christ, our Lord. Amen.

The Back Roads Of Advent

Matthew 1:20-24. *"But just when he had resolved to do this, an angel of the Lord appeared to him in a dream and said, "Joseph, son of David, do not be afraid to take Mary as your wife, for the child conceived in her is from the Holy Spirit. She will bear a son, and you are to name him Jesus, for he will save his people from their sins." All this took place to fulfill what was spoken by the Lord through the prophet: "Look, the virgin shall conceive and bear a son, and they shall name him Emmanuel," which means, "God is with us." When Joseph awoke from sleep, he did as the angel of the Lord commanded him."*

I was born and raised an urban pedestrian. I know that if you keep turning right four times in a row, you will get back to where you started. It works even if you keep turning left. You have gone "around the block."

In the suburbs and in the country, there are no such rules. My son is a Connecticut Yankee, born and raised. I had to teach him the "around the block" concept. But he taught me how to notice where trails cross in the woods, and he negotiates our suburban developments of terraces and cul-de-sacs with ease.

Sometimes I miss the "blocks." But I have become quite comfortable with "country" life.

When I am driving along a main drag, I try to notice the back roads and the side roads. Every now and then I see the same name recur, and I remember it for next time, then I take a side trip on the back road. I have found a whole collection of side roads that do that, though my current favorite is Flirtation Drive. That one even turns out to be a shortcut! Whether short cut or longer ramble, often I discover something on a side road. A lovely silo rises up out of the trees and an old farmstead is there, or a meadow, or a horse grazing... and then with that refreshing glimpse of something special, I am back on the main road, on my way again.

Mary and Joseph made their journey. Matthew told us Joseph fell in with God's plan and went up from Galilee, from the city of Nazareth, to

But Mary Kept All These Things

Judea and Bethlehem, a journey of about eighty miles. The roads were probably crowded with pilgrims like them, getting to the right place for the Roman census, and with Mary pregnant, Joseph might have tried a few quiet back roads off the beaten track, just for the peace of it. But on the other hand, with Mary pregnant, he might have done what we all do when we have a long way to go and a short time to get there: just stay on the road, and proceed in the steady stream of traffic until you reach your destination.

We know he got her there, and despite the crowds and lack of rooms, he found a safe place in a stable.

Do you want to get to Bethlehem? If so, just follow the shepherds. They know how to get to Bethlehem, for it is home. They know the back roads, the short cuts. But they don't know just which stable will hold the babe, do they? They know the road to town, but I like to think that it was off on a side road, on a quiet little-traveled road, that they found what they were looking for. They found a child and Mary and Joseph, just as the angels had promised them. They found a baby that would be named Jesus as the angel of the Lord had told Joseph all those months ago, "name him Jesus, for he will save his people from their sins." His people. That's us.

The Advent promise suggests that whenever we have lost our way, he will save us. When in our frightened cynicism we have been hesitant to try newness, whenever we have been given the wrong directions and paid attention to them, when we have listened to the wrong people, been led by the wrong motives, or sought the wrong goals, he will save us. When we've been too proud to ask directions or advice or help; when we have not listened to the advice of the people who love us, he will save us. That is the Advent promise for all pilgrims looking for Bethlehem.

The promise exists even when we have simply taken a wrong turn for all the wrong reasons and even when we have done it for the right reasons. It persists when we have no excuses, and when we have gone wrong. It remains whenever we have sinned, barreling down life's numbered highways oblivious, worried, stressed, or guilty. He will save us. "He will save his people from their sins." Jesus will save us with the manger and the straw, with the wood and the nails, and with the death.

Perhaps you might find a time or a place to turn aside this Advent. I know, on your journeys, you have seen side roads before, you may even have tried one and caught a glimpse of a sagging roof, or an image of joy, love, or fun. Of course, more often we have sped by, intent on our destination, fueled by envy, by depression, by pride. Why not turn aside

31

this very week? You've just read my account of the shepherds and their back road. Why not take a back road or two of your own this Advent?

Come, Lord, in whatever way you choose, straight through or by a back road. Get through to us even today and prepare us to receive your entrance into our lives this holy season. We pray in the name of the one who is coming, Jesus Christ our Lord. Amen.

Ox, Donkey, And Bream

Luke 2:7. *"... and laid him in a manger, because there was no place for them in the inn."*

In Advent, if it's cold, we bundle up. We get ready to stay warm, to lean over the manger, like a latter day shepherd. The infant slumbers, the stars glimmer like coals under a fire that is almost spent, but not quite. There is warmth, glow, and promises. We look forward to this so very much.

This Christmas, when it finally comes, wouldn't you gladly trade any two of your still-to-be-opened gifts to feel present, to be surrounded by that warmth, that glow, the possibility of that promise? Maybe three presents....

Whether our bodies actually bend or muscles move on Christmas or not is unimportant. We are truly anticipating entering the stable, lingering there to catch a glimpse of the child. Lingering to look inside, to enter. And then he, the smallest one, the baby, will reach out to you....

In the thirteenth century, a young friar named Francis also yearned for the presence of Christ at Christmas to feel real. He may have been the first person to create the idea for what we take for granted — a manger scene. His visits to the holy land (yes, imagine what a trek that would have been in the thirteenth century) may have inspired him. He went to a wealthy nobleman back in Italy, in Greccio in Umbria in 1223, almost 800 years ago, and asked for the loan of some land off the road, a quiet glen surrounded by sheltering hills. There he built a rough-hewn stable with a manger in it with straw and recruited a young couple to stand in for Mary and Joseph; and others to bring sheep from their family farms and act like shepherds for the night. He went to his noble friend again, John, and asked to borrow, as he put it, "an ox and an ass, I want it to feel like a stable, like the stable where the Lord was born, with animals nearby, I want to hear the sound of their breathing."

And so, Francis of Assisi, in nearby Greccio in 1223 created the first manger scene, the first Christmas crèche, the first, as the Italians call it, *precipio* with animals. Christmas Eve Mass was held there when the time came. He chose an ox and a donkey. They are not mentioned in the gospels, Francis decided on them. What kind of animals would you have chosen if you were that poor young friar, wanting to bring a gentle true message of faith to towns around your home?

We have a manger scene at home. We set it it up in Advent. Some folks don't put the baby in the manger until Christmas, but our manger and child are one piece. Every year for almost forty years we have added something quirky or special to the scene in addition to the shepherd's sheep and the ox and the donkey that came with it glued to the floor of the stable. The whole collection, almost forty years' worth, gathers around the crèche. They are not to scale; one Irish pottery sheep is taller at the shoulder than the top of Joseph's staff. There is an ivory chess piece bishop from Norway and a blue hippo from my son via the Metropolitan Museum of Art, a porcelain German Shepherd dog from my grandmother and a black cat from a wine bottle. Cows, horses, and a brightly colored wooden parrot — a turkey, a goose, a matador, a trout, a flamingo, a rooster, and a huge deer with enormous antlers are all there. And a caribou, I think. He is our most recent acquisition.

I like "Lagoon," a Christmas poem by a Russian who came to America and also spent a great deal of time living in Venice. My wife and I loved our visit to Venice, as he clearly loved the city… He wrote the poem in 1973 with a humble crèche in mind: "boats that rock from side to side, and the humble bream" (a kind of fish) guarding the manger, "not ass and oxen." Joseph Brodsky knew that someone needs to guard the presence of the Son of God in our lives so he placed bream there in place of ass and oxen.

There is no 'in place of' in my mind, the more the merrier are waiting at the manger in our house. Ox, donkey, and bream (I let the trout stand in for the Venetian species) and a caribou, guarding the Savior with warmth, all though Advent, keeping faith in his promises, to free us from our sins, teach us to love, and to restore us to wholeness.

The truth is that we will be there too when the days of Advent dwindle down. In ways that Francis knew well for himself, people have always wanted to include themselves among the believers waiting for that holy night, and the ox and the donkey have come to represent that.

In that, Francis made an inspired choice. The early Christians, in writing of the manger quoted the Old Testament prophet Isaiah: "The ox knows its owner and the ass knows the manger of its Lord, but my people do not know me." With Isaiah and Francis and the next centuries of believers, creating, painting, sculpting, standing in front of Christmas crèches all through these Advent days of preparing homes and hearts, we can see the ox and the donkey, sometimes portrayed in paintings with human faces, sometimes standing in for all who will believe, sometimes crowded in with a veritable Noah's ark of figures.

We stand next to them and they stand next to us, waiting. The bream, the ox, the donkey, the shepherds, even Mary and Joseph. They have all become toy figures made of clay or plastic, stone or wood, glass or straw — and we are huge compared to them.

Yes, "all this, in Bethlehem was of greater size" as Brodsky reminds us in another poem called "Presipio." Yet, all through Advent it feels right and good to be remembering. We bend down, we peer in, with believers from every corner of the cosmos to see this little show, and we yearn to see and to know and to believe. Because it is real.

Look. Listen. In these Advent moments recall that night. The holy family was at peace and smoke from their fire, like vanishing guilt, slipped out the door of the world, swept away by the promise of forgiveness, lying on the straw. There was, I think, a heavenly sigh heard, just as Francis hoped, from the donkey, or maybe it was the ox. One of us believers sighed. Such a sign in Advent would be like a prayer of waiting. Awaiting the warmth of love, the promise of forgiveness. Waiting is faithful. So is sighing.

Our Lord, we look around as we wait. We notice the unusual. Things seem strange sometimes. Grant us a quiet confidence in your power and enter our lives. Even as we wait for our presents, may we wait well for your presence. Amen.

Bethlehem Comes Complete

Matthew 2: 4-6 *"And calling together all the chief priests and scribes of the people, he inquired of them where the Messiah was to be born. They told him, "In Bethlehem of Judea; for so it has been written by the prophet: 'And you, Bethlehem, in the land of Judea, are by no means least among the rulers of Judah; for from you shall come a ruler who is to shepherd my people Israel'."*

We are waiting for the story of Jesus Christ to begin this Advent. It began in Nazareth with Mary and Gabriel, but the ensuing action happens in Bethlehem, and Bethlehem completes the story in a stable, in a manger, and in the adjacent fields, where shepherds are watching their flocks in the dark of night.

Bethlehem, city of David. The place where, 1,000 years before, the prophet Samuel came to look at the lineup of Jesse's sons and chose the youngest, the shepherd David, to become king of Israel and supplant Saul. Other places are certainly associated with David, as other places are certainly associated with Jesus; Jesus "of Nazareth," baptized in the Jordan River, water to wine was his first miracle in Cana; the sermon on the mount, overlooking the Sea of Galilee, crucifixion and resurrection in Jerusalem.

But this is the real beginning. It happens in Bethlehem. Bethlehem comes complete. In a stable, with a manger, and in the fields, shepherds watching their flocks by night — and angels come to sing for joy. Even as Jesus in the manger is the sign of God for God's people, Bethlehem is the beginning, the home place.

I've heard modern cowboys in New Mexico talk about home as their home place — whether they still live there or not, the home place is the place where promises are valued, remembered, solemnized, validated. The place that all-but-forgotten promises are remembered, solemnized, and validated. Bethlehem is our faith's original home place.

No matter where you live or have lived and no matter how far you may have wandered from home or your home place, yearning for angels, or even having forgotten angels altogether you have been called home for a reason. No matter how many addresses you can remember or recite — "782 East 32nd Street in Brooklyn, New York, 1100 East 55th Street in Chicago, Illinois, Gorman Road and Darby Road in Brooklyn, Connecticut, 33 Melody Court and 71 Davis Road in Fairfield, Connecticut, and 501 Lovely Street here in Avon" — no matter where you have heard others sing for joy, Bethlehem trumps them all. You and I, this Advent, have been called home for this all-but-forgotten promise. We are, like the shepherds, on our way this Advent, to our home place.

The shepherds can be one of our role models this Advent. They heard, they saw, they came, and they left. It was a glimpse of their salvation, *"good news of a great joy for all the people, for to you is born this day in the city of David ... and this will be a sign for you, you will find a babe, wrapped in swaddling clothes and lying in a manger."*

They, like us, prepared for meeting him, and then glorified and praised God for all they had heard and seen, as it had been told them. As we will, I trust.

Can you remember all that you have seen and heard about Christmas already this Advent? Can you think of a couple of ways that you and yours might just glorify God for what you will see and hear? Things like healing, laughter, parents, family, children, birthdays, baptisms, the fun gifts at Christmas, the trains, the bikes, the skis....

The shepherds left and it became for them an all-but-forgotten memory. The memory of Christmas and Bethlehem will be all-but-absent from the gospel records of Jesus' ministry. The shepherds will not appear again in print in the New Testament.

But did the shepherds forget? Do you think they could have? Do you remember any of your trips to Bethlehem's home place? Bethlehem, complete with its shepherds, its trees, its stockings, its presents, its carols, its candles; the warmth, the trust, the believing, the singing — did they forget? Remember, once, perhaps not so long ago, a gift you gave was received and opened with a smile or a tear, and yet not one word was spoken? Feel again that sure and certain confidence that God had entered your life, and welcomed you to a new wholeness, a new enfolding by the Spirit's grace, a new strengthening of faith, a brand new beginning. Remember — and wait for it to happen again this Advent.

Here's the deal: Nothing is missing this Advent. Bethlehem will come complete like a top-of-the-line kit. Like the stable I made for my son forty years ago from a small wooden fruit crate, with Mary and Joseph and the baby in a manger, it is complete. Perhaps it has some sheep and a shepherd — and even a nail to hang a hovering angel.

Bethlehem comes complete, with food. All different, yet each authentic to your home place... Viennese crescents, cut-out cookies, beef, turkey, ham, goose, lingonberries, Asian food, or the Feast of the Seven Fishes....

Bethlehem comes complete with a soundtrack. How many of the carols that you will sing could you actually close your eyes and sing the first stanza, and maybe the refrain, by heart, from memory? How many more contemporary singers will echo in your ears as you wrap or bake or decorate the tree — The Muppets, The Irish Tenors, or Mary Chapin Carpenter... all form precious memories of the Bethlehem home place for me.

Bethlehem comes complete, with presents — some get toys, in piles, all wrapped; some get gift cards, some get mittens or hats. Some will play happily with memories from years gone by, of a special person or a special gift. But even that will be enough.

For the beginning can be remembered again. The all-but-forgotten promise can be recalled, remembered, and trusted once again. That is the power of Advent promise to "all the people..."

I set down these words in their first draft just three blocks from Washington Square Park in Greenwich Village, near NYU. Inside the little restaurant, a little boy and his mother were speaking French in the seats next to me at the counter. The blue book of Christmas poems I was paging through (for my fifth Advent) was written by Brodsky — a Russian who loved to spend time in Venice as I mentioned in yesterday's reading. The busboy who brought me my espresso was from Ecuador; I ordered pasta carbonara, and the kind man who has become my friend over the years brought it and poured my prosecco. Dennis worked in the same general area for thirty years... Outside people were walking by speaking English, Arabic, German, Spanish, and Hebrew; and gesturing in the unmistakable language of New York City. Back home in Avon Connecticut, the voices I hear are accented with the intonations of the Midwest, Boston, Atlanta, Brooklyn, New Jersey, Michigan, and California; with roots in Italy, England, Ireland, Germany, Sweden, Finland, Norway, Portugal, Hungary, Iran, India, Pakistan, you name it....

A great joy for all the people — again, soon, as Advent works its way with us, again Bethlehem will indeed be complete. Soon the Christ will be born, yet again. In the Bethlehem of our hearts... and with the shepherds we will give thanks... I plan on doing just that. I hope that you will find ways to join me, for weeks to come. To find a way to give thanks to God, for the beginning of a story that comes complete.

Come, Lord, enter our lives with the power and gentle reminders that undergird your promises. The work has begun within us; all we need is gently arriving. The power of Bethlehem will be complete again. Fill us with thanks, through Jesus Christ, the ruler who will shepherd your people. Amen.

The Gift For You

Matthew 2:10-11. *"When they saw that the star had stopped, they were overwhelmed with joy. On entering the house, they saw the child with Mary his mother; and they knelt down and paid him homage. Then, opening their treasure chests, they offered him gifts of gold, frankincense and myrrh."*

Advent can point us toward one fact of our faith. What we are anticipating this Advent is a gift. It is all a gift, from start to finish, Even without thinking about gold, frankincense, and myrrh. A gift to Mary and Joseph, a son for their lives, but in the amazing circumstances of his birth, it can also become a gift of deep trust in the power and the glory of God for us.

Heaven knows, we know what to do with such a gift. First, we ascertain that it is for us. We read the tag, or someone we know and trust places it in our hands. In my wife's family, her grandfather would walk around distributing the gifts, reading the tags as we all sat in the circle that the furniture provided, in that crowded living room in Brooklyn. Getting the right gift is important. Our son Ryan began filling that role for us when he was quite young; he would gather a gift from beneath the tree, read the tag, and create piles of gifts, for Mom and Dad and for himself. (I think that was when he figured out that we actually had names, Ruth and Bill, not just Mom and Dad...). He always got the right gift in front of the correct person, even when Grandma and Aunt Helene and Uncle Tom came to celebrate with us.

To place a gift in front of the person it is intended for requires the trust of the group. Trust me when I declare that one of the great honors of being a parent, or a pastor, is to proclaim the truth of God's love – that the gift of the Savior is "for you." This Advent, try to get your mind around the fact that the gift is for you.

Knowing you got the gift intended for you, what's next? You open it up and see what it is. You lock eyes, and shout "Thanks!" across the room with a jumble of hugs and kisses, everyone striving to do their thanking or you call later, or write a note or text or email, or find another way... or maybe the thanking never gets done at all. Sometimes, that is part of the gift too.

You open it up, and then, of course, you use it. You wear it, you play with it, you cherish it, you find a place in your life, your closet, or your garage to keep it. This gift is from someone who knows you. The size is perfect, trust me. No need to stand in line to exchange it. You know from experience that if a gift is chosen well, it is a joy. God has chosen well for you!

It is all a gift, from start to finish. Advent is only the start, only the beginning. From Gabriel and Mary in Nazareth, to the shepherds, to the wise men in Bethlehem with gold and frankincense and myrrh, all the way to Mary and John at Golgotha... "Woman, here is your son... here is your mother." The wood of the manger, the wood of the cross — the dark warm space of the stable, and the dank dark emptiness of the tomb are a gift from start to finish. In our best moments, we come to believe that the gift is real, and we have faith to believe that in our lives, in our anxieties and our confrontations with sin, death, and the power of the devil. Somehow we are being offered a gift that can provide us with comfort and joy. Jesus is the gift, chosen and delivered. Jesus teaches a way of human happiness, not human adversity. His is a way of enough and more, not prosperity and anxiety.

So, prepare this Advent to receive this gift. It is for you. And once you receive it, unwrap it, and in the power of the love of God, sing along in your mind, by way of thanks, for God's gift and God's promises... *"God rest ye merry gentlefolk, let nothing you dismay, remember Christ our Savior was born on Christmas Day / to save us all from Satan's power when we were gone astray. Tidings of comfort and joy, comfort and joy. Tidings of comfort and joy."*

"The gift, for you!" announced and presented... "You're welcome!"

Eternal Lord, we hear the story of a star and people who follow. They bring gifts, although you are the gift. Help us to become people who recognize that the gift is for us; in gratitude, we wish to live lives of worship and love and service, even as we trust in your promises of comfort and joy. Amen.

You Don't Have To Choose

Matthew 2:1-3 *"In the time of King Herod, after Jesus was born in Bethlehem of Judea, wise men from the East came to Jerusalem, asking, "Where is the child who has been born King of the Jews? For we observed his star at its rising and have come to pay him homage." When King Herod heard this, he was frightened, and all Jerusalem with him."*

It is cold in the winter where I live in New England. For me it is often just a quick dash from the car to my front door or into the garage.

But when you are a pedestrian, it can get cold. Much colder than one realizes. We often miss that in the suburbs, but walking down the farm lane to get the mail from the rural delivery box, or making your way on foot from place to place in a city, the cold can really enter into you. There is a Norwegian saying that "there is no bad weather, there is only bad clothing." Sometimes though, I get cold.

I remember one of my solo day trips to New York City. It was a very cold day, an Advent day. And I walked blocks and blocks from the warm museum to an Italian restaurant I had heard about from a friend. As I sat there, it was warm again, but the cold had entered deep into me. The day's special was mushroom risotto, a kind of thick, hot, heavy rice/pasta offering that, in a restaurant like this, would be made from scratch and I chose it happily, anticipating, in an Advent kind of way, the warm comfort food entering my body soon and warming me from within.

The waitress asked, "Would you like anything to drink?" "I would." I replied, "A glass of red wine, from Italy." "We have two," she said, "by the glass. A Primitivo and a Chianti Classico, but it's not a Reserva." As I thought about this choice, I must have had a troubled look on my face, for she ran ahead and said: "Would you like to have a taste of each to help you decide?" What a good idea. It helped me to choose.

But we don't have to choose in Advent. Advent offers all of it. Advent offers additions, accretions, and miracles. Where shall we look for these miracles? Almost any place. Which place? Bethlehem, in Palestine, Manhattan or Detroit in America; Greccio in Italy... how about Sweden? Okay, Sweden.

In Sweden in the fourteenth century, a faithful woman who came to be known much later as Saint Bridget of Sweden, wrote of Jesus' sudden appearance on the ground: naked, enveloped in a glow of light. Jesus Christ, the light of the world, lying there on the hem of Mary's robe. I saw the painting in the museum. I was thinking about that picture as I put the fork into my risotto, and I felt the cold again...

I took another bite and recalled that a hundred years before Saint Bridget had her image of a Swedish winter and a naked baby in the light, Saint Francis of Assisi offered the world the very first manger scene. His creche, his *presipio*, was set up in the hills above Greccio in Italy, as you know. It had all the traditional earthy reality of Mary and Joseph, the shed, the stable, the manger, and the rustic shepherds in the distance, hearing the words and the song from the angels, the messengers of God. It has always felt warmer to me. At least Jesus was wrapped in swaddling clothes...

Mystical light or born when the time came for her to be delivered, perhaps even with a midwife on the edge of the story; was the child swaddled or naked? We don't need to choose. Our Advent perspective shows us things beyond the center. Connections abound — this is the time when the whole world plays carols, in a multitude of languages, when folks plan to push mismatched tables together as family and friends gather from far and near to be together.

So, in our Advent busyness, what are we preparing for? Warmth or chill? Scandinavian Sweden or Mediterranean Italy? Shepherds or wise men, angels or a star? Perhaps both. Sheep or camels or both? "*Wrapped in swaddling clothes and lying in a manger*," or held in Mary's arms in the light of Joseph's lantern; or lying in a nimbus of light on the hem of Mary's extraordinary gown? You don't have to choose. You can have it all, in Advent. Connections abound, options for images of Advent faith are strewn everywhere.

Behind all the choices, in the midst of the multiplicity of miracles that have touched your life this past year, in spite of the collection of calamities that may have shaken you to the core of your faith this past year, behind, beneath, and present though every blessing and every calamity is the promise that Advent keeps warm, even in the coldest winter.

Even for those who are hungry, or know another kind emptiness. In Advent, anticipating the Child, the mere thought of darkness can remind us of Saint Bridget and the image of bringing light as if out of nowhere. We need that reminder. So often we see the signs that Herod reigns, but the stronger he is, the more sure, the more certain the wonder of Jesus birth. The constancy of this faith is the solid ground of Advent hope. In Advent, we are all of us wise men, on a journey to the true King, and with the shepherds we have just kindled our fires... perhaps lit the second candle on an Advent wreath.

It doesn't really matter what you choose to order from your Christmas menus, whatever you will labor over in your kitchen, no matter what beverage will be poured out to accompany your meal. It doesn't matter.

I know that everything seems to matter to us. It can even drive us to distraction. But the sea of change in Advent thinking is to realize again that we matter to God. You matter. God loves you. God is sending his son to be the light of the world — your world. The light that glints in a glass of wine or a Dr. Pepper® as you hold it up to a bright window, that is Christ's nimbus. So is that love light in the eyes of your children, your grandchildren. The still, bubbling or blinking lights that decorate your tree, be they white or of many colors. The ancient light from the star that guided the wise men, or the smoky glimmer of the shepherds' campfires as they watched their flocks by night.

Whether you are on the move or trying to be still in your watching and waiting — it doesn't matter. I believe you simply will not make it through the remaining weeks of Advent without any number of opportunities to catch a glimpse of God's gift, if you watch patiently for it and realize it is about you. Christ is coming. He is the light for your darkness — no matter the weather. Ready?

Heavenly Father, we give you our thanks for the opportunities that are scattered in the midst of our everyday lives. We are grateful for the shining light of your son, the true word of life coming into our world. Shine today in our eyes, and awaken us to the grace and truth of our faith. Amen.

Invited Guests

Luke 2:1-3 *"In those days a decree went out from Caesar Augustus that all the world should be enrolled. This was the first enrollment, when Quirinius was governor of Syria. All went to their own towns to be registered."*

The lines from John Lennon and Paul McCartney in the song, "In My Life" lead us to questions. Look up the lyrics on the web. Are there places we remember? Where are they? Why do we remember them? Are there places you remember preparing for Christmas? Of course there are.

Those are places that you remember all your life, even though some have changed, and some remain. The corner, the hill, the shop where you first got to handle the tree with your family or the first time you had a hand in baking or decorating the Christmas cookies. Where was that kitchen? I remember those Advent moments in my life.

I am very blessed to remember Bethlehem itself. On my second pilgrimage to the holy land, there were Bavarian tourists singing "Stille Nacht" in the grotto beneath the Church of the Nativity, while my wife Ruth and I stood there, holding hands, gazing at the seventeen-pointed silver star on the floor that marks the spot where tradition says the manger sat. That is the same manger with the Christ Child. I believe that whether you have been to Bethlehem on a tour of the Holy Land or not, you remember Bethlehem too, especially at Christmas.

Joseph remembered Bethlehem. It was his home place, and because of the emperor's tax census he had to return there with Mary to register. Luke located it in time: "In those days a decree went out from Caesar Augustus that all the world should be enrolled." In those days....

Indeed, in these days, you can remember the paths you have been taking on your own journeys toward Bethlehem this year. Through crowded shopping malls, across the shadowlands of illnesses. Whether we are beset by celebrations or concerns, we always travel with Mary, Joseph and with God. God travels wonderful paths with human beings.

But Mary Kept All These Things

With Mary and Joseph we have been roused from our present lives, our present painful or pleasant places this Advent, and are moving toward Bethlehem. Although God's invitation simply spreads out and enfolds Bethlehem, it doesn't stop there; God's love enfolds other places too. It enfolds the places where we are doing whatever we do: buying a tree with Dad or placing a chocolate kiss on a just-out-of-the-oven peanut butter cookie. It can happen to you, exactly as the invitation enfolded the shepherds that first Christmas as they were simply doing what they did: watching their flocks by night.

To them in their place and to you and me in our places, the loving invitation comes. I promise. There will be room to bring yourself inside the story.

You can see that in nativity scenes from around the world. We've collected crèches for a while now. We put them up every Advent. Lots of figures show up in addition to the holy family, such as shepherds, and the wise men. One from Germany has Santa Claus kneeling at the manger, and on the other extreme, one from Central America has a figure of Satan, turning, as if in fear, away from the Child.

It is a fact of our faith that no one is forgotten, no one is alone, and you may invite anyone you want to join you. People you cherish, folks you remember, even the little drummer boy or your college roommate, your current boyfriend, your old boyfriend, the uncle who could recite "The Night Before Christmas" from memory, the young friend who died last month, or your son's great-grandfather who died forty years ago, whose Bible is still the one our family reads from each Christmas dinner — all are invited. You can choose to invite someone who is special to you. Your memory gives you that gift and that power.

Don't forget, the shepherds were just roustabouts; ragged, not important in the world's eyes. They worked outdoors, unsheltered, just as we are unsheltered from the worries and toils and cares of our lives. The shepherds were invited by angels. Wise men from the east followed a star and saw it as their invitation to make the journey. They arrived later, just like you and me, who will arrive later still, at our own Bethlehem place, this place we remember. It is this place at the end of our Advent path that enfolds us. It is this place that remains, no matter what. Remember that you are invited.

Look up those lyrics and read them carefully one more time.

Bethlehem remains. Forever and for always and for peace and for forgiveness and for joy and for love and for faith. Forever and ever. Bethlehem remains.

But Mary Kept All These Things

Come, Lord, be with us even now. Thank you for the promise of the wondrous birth that is the path to so much newness. Help us to follow your path, through joy and struggle, bring us to new life ourselves in the Bethlehem of our hearts. Help us to remember the power of faith. Amen.

Surprise Me...

John 1: 6-13. *"There was a man sent from God, whose name was John. He came as a witness, to testify to the light, so that all might believe through him. He himself was not the light, but he came to testify to the light. The true light, which enlightens everyone, was coming into the world. He was in the world, and the world came into being through him; yet the world did not know him. He came to what was his own, and his own people did not accept him. But to all who received him, who believed in his name, he gave power to become children of God, who were born, not of blood or of the will of the flesh or of the will of man, but of God."*

We are in the thick of Christmas preparation. Advent helps us to count the days. Finding gifts and stocking stuffers, the tree, baking and candles in our windows, watching for 'Christmas Lights' in the neighborhoods we traverse; all can be joyful symbols of Christ's coming for those of us who know the power of his light. The impending arrival of "the true light" is not neglected, never forgotten or taken for granted.

For years, we hung a blue felt Advent banner that my wife made years before, with four tall white felt images of candles, and we added one more yellow felt flame each week with a straight pin. One year our family room got a new paint job and we were loath to hammer nails in the old places. The Advent banner has not been hung. But now, on the kitchen table there are four new round cut crystal tea light holders; they glow when the right number of candles are lit at dinner. One will still be just glass, no glow yet in the fourth one. Then, over supper, we will share a conversation or a memory or some words of anticipation, rooted in the coming light of the coming Christ. In our best moments, we unwittingly testify to the power of the light that is coming, all through Advent.

It helps us comprehend what a deeply wonderful time of year is upon us. A chill is in the air, and our sense of expectation grows, darker each and every day. Yet Christ is coming! Every now and then, I confess, I may be more than a little too preoccupied with my busyness: shopping, wrapping and the rest. But, every now and then, I find my busyness is redeemed from frustration by a reminder from John — "yet the world did not know him." For me, it is a moment of remembrance, of faith, perhaps a moment of gentle surprise. For in all our activities we are indeed, whether we have it in our minds or not — we are preparing to "receive the light…" we are "testifying to the light" like John... "the true light" that "is coming into the world." We are, in fact, preparing to receive him. God knows, and he knows that we "believe in his name."

Next year, we may get around to nails in the family room, and we will probably hang the banner. We will probably put those four cut-glass holders on the kitchen table too. The extravagance of God's love is like that, enough and more. Change by addition, and the new joins the old, and renews it, augments it, enriches it. Sometimes, more is just more. But in Advent, God's extravagance creeps into our heart.

You may be planning a Christmas journey, or expecting company or a phone call. You may be still deciding on the central element of a fine dinner surprise (I still recall the Christmas we had goose!) Perhaps you are anticipating bringing one special dish to be placed on a groaning table, surrounded by smiling faces you know well. You may be hoping this year to receive one perfect gift, part surprise, part "It's just what I wanted!"

We know pretty much who is coming to our house this Christmas Eve, and who will arrive the next day, in time for Christmas dinner with presents, laughter, and gratitude. But, remember, Mary and Joseph were surprised by the shepherds, who had earlier been surprised by the angels. May some sort of gentle surprise be a part of the power of this Advent present for you. It will happen well before Christmas if you keep Advent. You may not even realize it until later, but it will happen. It always does.

Don't get distracted by what seems the shadow side of this, of people not knowing or caring that he is coming. Rather, may you be wrapped in the warmth of your memories as well as in the expectant anticipation of wonderful new moments and promises yet to be imagined. Remember, Jesus Christ is the light of the world! May there be glimpses of this happy, joyful truth for you and yours this holy season of Advent. May the light of Christ illuminate our faces, our eyes and our hearts as we make our way through the shadows of modern living.

Perhaps there will be an unexpected delivery from the United Parcel Service, or the FedEx truck, or a phone call or Skype. Or perhaps you may experience a deeper interaction than you were expecting with the reality of your faith. Although the light is less each and every day this week and the days of preparation are dwindling down too, know this: the light is most certainly coming.

This Advent, may God's amazing Spirit surprise you with one piece of newness that renews your anticipation, and even if it seems at first that it doesn't quite fit in, give it a chance... may the sweet gentleness of it, (and it will be gentle, we pray) embrace and enfold you on your journey to yet another Christmas, and, as Christ arrives, as the light of his saving grace enters into your reality, may you know again the power that has made you a child of God. Own it, gently testify to the light in your life, be extravagant with your love this week. What shape could that extravagance take? Surprise me... well, no... surprise someone else....

Holy Father, as you prepare to show yourself to the world again, shine your light into our hearts today. Help us to see clearly the tasks before us, and keep us connected to the vast resources of your amazing power; Continue to guide us as we testify to your light in all we do. We pray in the name of the one who is coming, Amen.

Journeys Begin With Arrivals

Luke 2:20. *"And the shepherds returned, glorifying and praising God for all they had heard and seen, as it had been told them."*

Let's go on a journey, an adventure, a pilgrimage today! Airports, bus stations, train stations, highways, streets, and lanes are all crowded. Let's go! But don't forget, all journeys begin with arrivals.

It seems like Advent is a celebration of a journey and an arrival. Gabriel journeys and arrives in Nazareth to announce to Mary that she will bear a child. Mary traveled and arrived in the hill country to see her cousin Elizabeth, well along in her amazing pregnancy, and they rejoiced together at what God had done in their lives. Mary and Joseph trekked some eighty miles from Nazareth to arrive in Bethlehem. The wise men were on the move, and Santa Claus too.

A young man of my acquaintance — he is my age now — was in love — well, he still is, but it was just beginning then. The young man journeyed on Christmas Eve to be with his beloved, to celebrate with her. It was a long journey halfway across a city. Four neighborhoods at least, on two different busses. And he arrived on time. It was as wonderful as he remembers it, carols and candles in church with coffee after and presents shared by her extended family. Even one for him.

And then, even though he had arrived, it was time to begin the journey back, back across the neighborhoods, it was time to return. Outside the apartment, he said, he looked up at the window and shouted "Merry Christmas!"

They still talk about that journey back. He left alone, as he had arrived, and it was snowing; a blizzard, he said. It was about one o'clock in the morning, he knew there was no sense in waiting for the bus.

Sometimes when he tells the story he walked all the way back, more than three hours through the dark, cold, snowy streets. Sometimes in the story, a car stopped and took him most of the middle of the way home. It would have been nice and warm in the car, and the middle-aged couple who picked him up asked about his plight and he told them. "You must

51

really love her," they said. Sometimes the story seems heroic.

But he never tells the story, unless you really beg him. He knows it was not heroic. She tells it with a quiet smile. Her family tells it with awe. His family tells it with incredulity, thinking it must be an exaggeration. "How far could it have been after all?" "Was it really all that cold?"

He said, "No, it wasn't that far, it wasn't that cold." Not when you figure in the love. He never felt he had an option, it was important to arrive, to be with her, even though he knew he had to return. It was the price of love. Without the love of course it is quite a ridiculous journey, even foolish.

From heaven above to earth, Christ came to a stable in Bethlehem. And then journeyed back — after the Christmas arrival, the trek to Calvary. The manger dismantled and fitted out for a cross. The anguish endured. All for love.

For love of you and me, and the young man and his girlfriend, and eventually their son — and now, for their granddaughter too. It is even for their extended families and your families too — even the in-laws. For us all. He arrived in Bethlehem on that first Christmas, and then his journey began. Mostly that is true for us too. When you and I think we have finally arrived, more often than not, our journey has just begun.

When I first visited Bethlehem in the holy land, in 1992, we all filed in to the Church of the Nativity from the bus. We walked down a set of stairs, into the grotto where the cave commemorated as the site of the manger and the birth is located; underneath the chancel of that ancient church.

I hung back and was the last one in. We all sang "Silent Night" and then our wonderful Palestinian guide, Theo, looked over at me and said, "Reverend Carter, would you offer a prayer?" And I did, although I was quite surprised and unprepared. I prayed. But what I remember most is how wonderful it felt in that moment to be asked for a favor, unexpectedly. Now, I will ask you for a favor.

Remember the trip that comes after. I ask you to remember the trip that comes after the arrival at Bethlehem. Remember God's arduous journey in Christ from Bethlehem to Calvary, to the Mount of the Ascension. Such a far journey for the love of you. Please try your best to be attentive to your own trips back after arriving somewhere. Wherever you go in these Advent days, be attentive on the way back.

Sometimes it may feel as if you must walk the whole, cold way back alone. Sometimes someone will warmly stop and give you a ride part of the way, or perhaps keep you company and simply ease your difficulty, and interrupt the loneliness of that particular journey. Sometimes you will be the one to stop and forget your own struggles as you help someone else with theirs.

May it be a journey steeped in faith, an adventure in trusting God, a pilgrimage steadied by a staff of believing; praying and picking a way through the sorrow, the joy, the anxiety to a place of quiet confidence, journey in love. Speak out of love. Act out of love. Choose gifts and exchange them out of love. The journey that begins with his arrival has no meaning unless there is love.

Prepare us, O God, for the coming of our Lord. We are filled with expectation. Help us to be ready. Fill us with strength for our journey. May we arrive to hear Christ's Word, see his light and then return to live his love for all to see. Amen.

Be Not Afraid
(A Remembrance of September 11, 2001)

Matthew 2:16-18. *"When Herod saw that he had been tricked by the wise men, he was infuriated, and he sent and killed all the children in and around Bethlehem who were two years old or under, according to the time that he had learned from the wise men. Then was fulfilled what had been spoken through the prophet Jeremiah: 'A voice was heard in Raman, wailing and loud lamentation. Rachel weeping for her children; she refused to be consoled, because they were no more.'"*

All during the Advent season. after the sorrows of September 11, 2001, I remember the dark subterranean waiting. Waiting for December 24 to come and wondering what I could possibly say on that Christmas Eve, a generation ago now. The Matthew text above is the one I preached on that Sunday, September 16, 2001. The words below helped shape my message that Sunday morning. They still ring true for me today, and I hope that they affirm the same message today, for you....

The dark waiting was almost over. The Advent candles on the wreath had been lit, one by one, one at a time, and it culminated that night, when everyone would hold a candle, but the darkness was still lapping at the edges.

"Don't be afraid," I wrote. "We have been a long time this fall looking for the light, against the pull of danger and darkness, looking for a safe place. In the aftermath of the tragedy of September 11, no place has seemed safe, except maybe the hillsides of home. And sometimes it has seemed like there is no clear direction home."

Many people across the country can still remember that morning; we began to mourn, we were certainly feeling frightened. We were captured by those images of chaos at the Pentagon in Washington, and the sad, sad wreckage of bravery in a field in Pennsylvania. We heard the stories and watched the coverage of people walking; heroic searchers and rescuers walking up to help, while others were streaming down to safety. And as we watched and as we listened, our hearts joined the streams of people walking north on the avenues of New York City, and those trekking south over the Brooklyn Bridge — to a home, to a friend's home, to safety — anywhere — away. They were looking for a safe place.

Joseph was looking for a safe place too. A place away from prying eyes and the jostling shoulders of the growing crowds of registrants for Caesar's new census. (Who knew they would have to seek a safe place again, away from Herod's wrath?)

This Advent, we remember the first journey. Joseph and Mary had left Nazareth, the safety of the hills of home, to walk the long miles to his historic home place of Bethlehem. Mary endured the discomforts of late pregnancy, and now the pains were beginning, and with her modesty at stake — he finally found a stable. It was in a cave probably, a natural shelter in the limestone rocks of Bethlehem. Their walking and their waiting was almost over. She labored and bore a son and they called his name Jesus as the angel had instructed, what seemed like ages, and so many miles ago.

The shepherds were in a safe place too. They were on their familiar hillsides with their lambs, sheep, and goats; flocks that had been in their care for generations. From the vantage point above their hometown, they had watched the road streaming with pilgrims for the census — the bustle and the noise had frightened the flock and had been a real worry to the shepherds too, but now that all had settled in for the night, perhaps they dozed. Just a bit....

Then, the sky exploded and they were filled with fear.... "Do not be afraid," the angel challenged them. "Do not be afraid."

They went into the town, forsaking safety and trusting the promise of good news, although they were afraid. They were. They went in spite of their fear, and found the manger, the stable, the cave.

Imagine that midnight cave with the glowing embers of Joseph's well-laid fire as the only light left, and has filled the place with a thick warmth in the night. As we walk into the shadowy darkness, the warmth is almost a corporeal presence — almost a comfort for our fears, whatever they may be this Advent....

Imagine striking a match in that midnight cave, and seeing the farm tools, the animals, and we, we with the shepherds, are mute. Mute with what? Mute with terror, or is it expectation; still listening to the echoes of the angel's promises, even as we recall the prophet Jeremiah — and Rachel's refusal to be consoled.

God will send his consolation to us as surely as he sent an angel to the shepherds. God's message will come to you on your own dark hillsides, in the darkest nights of your despair. It will. This Advent, God is drawing us close again by a varied and amazing myriad of paths: need or faith, or custom, piety or pain. He is drawing us closer each day, in spite of the mid-winter darkness.

And in our darkness, as we strike our match to light another candle on another Advent wreath, we can almost make out the shape of what God wants us to do... who God wants us to be; as the match flares, we can clearly see the truth of his love for us. For the child's eyes are open; and we will see him as he was and is and will be forever — powerful and full of light. Even in the deepest hours of the night his eyes flash with a brightness that says, "Fear not. I am Jesus. I will bring your consolation. I will comfort you. I will save you."

Eternal Lord, we give you thanks for the coming of Jesus into our quiet world of shadowy fear and emptiness. He is the clear, bright, vibrant word of fullness. Thank you for the shining word of safety and life, which has come to us through Jesus Christ, your son, our Lord. Amen.

Christmas Postcards

Luke 2:6 *"While they were there, the time came for her to deliver her child."*

Ever notice how two people can look at the same event and have different memories later? Ever notice how reading or hearing the same story, people are moved to remember different images, elements or messages?

I read a short Christmas story by Donald Hall one Advent titled *Christmas at Eagle Pond*. It had only 78 pages. It was a memoir of sorts about his first long ago Christmas in the country. There are lovely images of presents and carol singing and Christmas dinner. But for me, the premier element that made a place to linger in my brain, was the story of 1940, when he was ten. At that time, postcards cost a penny and had a head of Ben Franklin where a stamp would be. His grandfather would walk each day to the country post office, with three penny postcards in hand, because every day Grandma wrote to her three grown daughters, and every day she had three postcards back.

I told that little story from the book to two of my pastor friends when we were sharing a breakfast out together that December. I gave a copy of the book to each of them as Advent gifts. One grew very quiet and said, "When I was a boy, my grandfather would send me a postcard every week, not every day but every week. It was special."

It is special, isn't it? So often, postcards are open moments for truth, for feelings, for stories, and for love you wish to share. Yes, I realize that anyone can read them, from the letter carrier, to postal sorters, to the clerk at the hotel if you mail them when you are out of town. But finally, the one you have chosen reads your words and smiles and feels loved.

The Christmas story is like that. So much so that I have begun to hope that postcards were sent during that first Christmas. I like to imagine that we can read them still as part of our Advent devotions....

The first postcard probably came from Joseph, who sent it back to his rabbi. "I couldn't find much of a place with Mary so close to delivering.

But Mary Kept All These Things

But we do have some privacy. It is not insufficient, it is fitting."

And then an angel's postcard... to God. "When all things were in quiet silence, and the night in its swift silence was half spent — your all powerful word leapt down from heaven's royal throne."

Joseph wrote a second card too, this one to his best friend back in Nazareth who was filling in for him at the carpenter's shop. "It's a boy! I had to clean out a manger and lay my cloak in it. Mary has swaddled our son... it's not the cradle I would have made, but he *is* sleeping!"

And Mary, to her mother, Anne: "I have a son! The angel was right those months ago, telling me not to be afraid. All is well. I love you."

Maybe a shepherd wrote a postcard to his sister in Jerusalem. "We have just kindled our fires. The sky is uncommonly clear and the stars are so bright. You would love it."

And finally another postcard, from the youngest shepherd to his father. "We shouldn't do it I suppose, but we're leaving to go into Bethlehem to see about something astonishing... wish us luck."

The core of Advent may just be anticipating the good news of God's presence, near us. Wrapped and swaddled in a place we can find when we need it most. Perhaps it is a smile or a feeling of being loved. A Savior, among us! He is with us in these Advent days. Good news for you and for me, and for how many others?

Postcards are open and honest. Postcards are visible for all to see, boiled down to just a few lines, similar to that first Christmas. Perhaps you could give it a try this Advent; a postcard and a stamp is still a pretty good value. What would you write on a postcard for Christmas? Who would most need to read the words you could write? Who is the person that you would most like to have a card from? What words would you most wish to read on the card that they would send to you?

Dear God, we look forward to Christ's coming. We remember your entry into our lives then, and we pray boldly for your arrival in the very midst of our lives now. We are joyous at the news. A child will be born. May our preparations find a quiet fulfillment as we share our love. Amen.

The Close and Holy Darkness

Luke 2:13-14. *"And suddenly there was with the angel a multitude of the heavenly host, praising God and saying, "Glory to God in the highest heaven, and on earth, peace..."*

The just-less-than-life sized handmade wooden manger, which made its way closer to the altar each Sunday of Advent when I served St. Matthew Lutheran Church in Avon, Connecticut, was in my arms. The hay still was pungent as I moved it a score of steps down the dark, chilly aisle one Monday morning. I was a bit distracted. I was thinking about the Dylan Thomas masterpiece "A Child's Christmas in Wales," which I had just re-read. It's a story of a six-year-old boy's memories of a very eventful Christmas full of aunts and uncles, as well as hunting cats (jaguars) with his friends with snowballs. They opined about "useful presents" like mufflers and hats or "useless presents" like painting books and false noses. There were carols, sweet jelly, and even a fire put out swiftly by frantic firemen. There was plenty of hub-bub. As I carried the manger down the aisle, my mind was a jumble of images, though the manger was still in my arms.

Sometimes I believe the manger seems magnetic — I'm not sure we always notice that. It moves to the center as Advent progresses and things clatter up and surround it. In my grandmother's home on Church Avenue in Brooklyn, New York, when I was a child, she created a scene underneath her Christmas tree. That scene was my favorite part of her Christmas home. I had never seen anything like it. There were ice skaters on a mirror pond, houses, trains, and delivery trucks; it was the hubbub of real life surrounding a classic little manger scene in the center. In my home, for years now, one of our half-dozen crèches was smack dab in the middle of a peculiar herd of animals that I describe much too often, but I can't help myself: flamingos, turkeys, a green aardvark, a bullfighter, a parrot, a raccoon, to name just a few in this day's reading. Almost every year a new animal or figure joins our menagerie. I always like to think the manger attracts them, all of them, all of us, and more....

But Mary Kept All These Things

This Advent, which means, *coming*, we look ahead with building expectation to what is coming. We know that Jesus is coming and will be born in the close and holy darkness and placed in a manger in a stable in the midst of noisy animals and an anxious, expectant, loving family. Jesus was tenderly placed, not in some nursery or a sanitary layette, but in a manger that Joseph probably cleaned out a bit, and perhaps topped off with some fresh straw. It was in the center of the hubbub, the center of attention — the center of life.

If we are to prepare to experience the coming birth of Christ this Advent, it may not be only in the readied guest rooms of our minds and lives but right in the center of it all. It may be in a manger in the middle of a mess. We will anticipate his coming birth into the midst of people who love each other, miss each other, as well as into the mess of people who sometimes misunderstand each other and even people who are estranged from one another too, perhaps for a good long time... or a bad long time.

I look forward to his moving right into the center of the pain of the world, where his influence still whispers in the face of the hostile din to, "Be reconciled, be healed, be forgiven, forgive, do unto others...". This Advent we yearn for him to come and be born in Bethlehem, and yes, in the Bethlehem of our hearts, as well as the first Bethlehem, in Palestine; where Jesus' voice still cries, echoing the angel's song — crying aloud for peace where there is none, and wherever there is no good will. That could be in the Middle East, in our hearts, in the center of the ache, or in the middle of the strife. Even in the midst of our disappointments and our fears, even in the loneliness of a close and holy darkness, he will come.

Perhaps it has been a long aching Advent season for you and yours. It would have been an anxious waiting for Mary, her first child and all. It was hard for Joseph in his uncertainty and then the long journey from Nazareth to Bethlehem. In the close and holy darkness of heaven, where the agony of what was in store for Christ was known, it was anguish.

In Advent, we prepare, as we can, for Jesus to come and to insert himself into the center of our lives, into the close and holy darkness of our prayers. "God from God, light from light, true God from true God" as the Nicene Creed would have it, "for us and for our salvation, he came down from heaven, the very glory of God, into the close and holy darkness of every dark night."

Carrying that wooden prop of a manger down the church aisle, it suddenly occurred to me that Dylan Thomas ended his "Child's

But Mary Kept All These Things

Christmas in Wales" on Christmas night, after the boy climbed into bed to go to sleep, with the whispering phrase, "I said some words into the close and holy darkness, and then I slept." I realized that morning, in the sanctuary, and have never forgotten it since, that I believe I have an idea exactly what that boy prayed. "Forget the guest room," he said, "Stay with me here — all night — all my life long." That's what he said. And that's what Jesus does. All night long, all your life long. Thank God.

Come Lord Jesus, visit us in our time. Grant to each of us the heart of a child which never ceases to marvel at your wonders, so that once again, you may find us watching and waiting in hope. We ask you this, because of your love for us. Amen.

Congratulations!

Luke 2:5. *"... to be enrolled with Mary, his betrothed, who was with Child."*

I would like to proclaim anew a part of the expectation of Christmas you have always known, to remind you of the gentle tugging insistence we all but forget each Advent.

We anticipate the journey to Bethlehem, no room in the inn, the stable, manger, the angels' song, the shepherds' haste, and Mary's pondering. We know the babe in the manger. We know he does not stay in the manger. He goes to the temple, to the wilderness, the Jordan, the Galilee, the upper room, the cross, and to Golgotha. We know he is risen from the dead. We know so much. But let's not run too far ahead this Advent. Let's move more slowly, to Mary, "who was with Child."

I wonder if anyone said congratulations to Mary or to Joseph. I wonder if anyone said congratulations to the artist Duccio in Siena in 1300. He was a father, that part is clear to me, even though I am not at all familiar with his biography. There's a painting at the Metropolitan Museum of Art in New York City. Duccio painted it in 1300, the Met bought it for 48 million dollars in 2004 — *A Madonna and Child*. It is singed along the bottom edge by devotional candles keep lit beneath it centuries ago. 48 million dollars and it is only eight by ten inches. Eight by ten inches for 48 million dollars.

She had picked him up out of the manger; he was not in swaddling clothes, he was in a reddish tunic of sorts — but here was the thing — here is the truth that we need to know and remember: the child was the active one. The child was reaching up to Mary, to grab her, to touch her, to get her attention.

That's what you look forward to I think when you are "with child." It begins, I suppose, when somebody says "Congratulations!" There are other remembered beginnings. I keep a small ultrasound image of my granddaughter in my prayer book at Psalm 139... "For it was you who formed my inward parts; you knit me together in my mother's womb."

But Mary Kept All These Things

For many years now, in Advent, I take a look in my sock drawer. A hospital mask, a plastic nail cleaner, and a plastic scrub brush, all from the delivery room preparation on the day my son was born. What memories of beginnings are in your sock drawer? Then of course, you remember the time when the child reached up from the manger, from the crib, the car seat, the floor; reached up and tugged on a scarf, or a nose, an ear, a finger, a mustache, or a necklace.

The destination of Advent is a place where God reaches into our lives with love, the unconditional love of a child. We wonder and worry, but God crosses the distance. The child reaches out and our lives are never the same. God goes looking for us long before we go looking for him. However we put it, and there are countless ways, God's love is there ahead of us, forgiveness is never a matter of persuading God of something, but rather discovering for yourself that there is no longer any distance to be traversed. God loves you and sends his son who reaches out for you, just as every child does, to touch your skin, your sin, your ear, your fear, your mustache, your finger, your necklace. *For Mary is with child and the child will be born.*

And this child, this Savior king, will reach out and up from the manger and touch us, and nothing will be the same. That's what so often happens when a child enters the scene. Hugh Grant's character in the movie *9 Months* finally sold his Porsche and bought a family sedan. In the middle of that night, after months of his personal Advent, after months of shameful refusal of responsibility, he held his child, who clung to him as Van Morrison sang on the stereo and awakened the mother… These are the days… they will last forever. These are the days — there's only here and now…."

God loves you, and he will send this tiny child, filled with great love, which will be Christmas. Oh, yes, congratulations! (In advance…).

God, gracious Lord of eternity, as we prepare our homes and hearts, we understand that Mary is with child. Fill us with anticipation and with the sure and certain faith that comprehends, that indeed, these are the days, and, indeed, they will last forever. Amen.

Delight And Disbelief

Luke 2:18 *"And all who heard it wondered at what the shepherds told them."*

Wonder can be a remarkable word. Verb or noun, we so often use it tepidly, with no consequence. "Is he telling the truth?" "I wonder..."

Consider the wonders of science or technology, of computers, iPhones, and the rest... from the early days of "You've got mail!" to the Instagram photos that let your friends show you what they're having for dinner in real time!

Some time ago, (in the era of "You've got mail!") I read the obituary of Kenneth Brugger, who died in 1998 at the age of eighty; who had been the discoverer of the monarch butterfly's winter lair. He found the solution to the lingering puzzle of the monarch butterflies' disappearance in the winter; he found them in Mexico. For many generations, researchers had wondered: "Where do they go?" Following his scientific trail, that had eluded so many researchers, on January 2, 1975, Ken found himself driving through a forest in Mexico, and the trees there were covered with millions of orange and black butterflies.... He found them. If you Google him, you will see that is his accomplishment. Finding the monarchs. He must have been struck with something like wonder as he drove, and then stopped, and then looked up and around him... and saw them.

It must have been close to wonder for him, yet it has little impact on our everyday lives I suppose, or our real future — in fact, the monarchs are now threatened and are in decline. The Mexican forests are much more bare, and our meadows and gardens are too.

Authentic wonder, it seems to me, is pretty hard to come by. Wonder — as in, to marvel; to be awestruck or possibly terrified, precisely as the shepherds were when heaven met earth in the message of the angel of the Lord on that hillside on the first Christmas.

Not on a screen, not on a highway eighty miles southwest of Mexico City driving through the mountains, but on a hillside in Bethlehem, long before your childhood; long before Mr. Brugger's childhood too.

To wonder is to be seized by delight and disbelief simultaneously. "It's so wonderful, I just can't believe it!" To wonder is also to be overwhelmed by something brand new, even as you are reminded of, and in touch with, everything you have ever experienced before, juxtaposed, lying adjacent but all too often neglected in your mind.

Isn't each Advent meant to be exactly like that? Perhaps you buy one new ornament for your tree each year, or maybe it will be your first Christmas with a new baby or a new dog — yet in the very same moment you can feel all the Christmases past washing over you... children now grown are tiny again... Special uncles, aunts, or beloved grandparents now gone, are somehow present. There is delight and disbelief... and wonder.

Recall the wonder, this Advent; remember coming downstairs as a child, or watching your children come into the room where the tree was now decorated, lit with colored lights, (or were they white, or perhaps those ones that bubble?) and underneath the tree the childhood miracle of abundant presents — toys... and you can see the wonder of it all. Yes, you just let it wash over you. You had to. You have to. And you can again. Anticipating that wonder *is* the power of Advent.

You see, you and I, we don't master the source of wonder. Rather, you and I, in our best moments, we grow still in the presence of wonder and let it overtake us. Overwhelm us, in the best and gentlest of ways. Because after all, this is about what God is doing — not what we have done or will do, or even wish we could do all our decorations and our gifts and our smiles notwithstanding!

The truest measure of Advent, and the coming Christmas, is in what God is doing. Therein lies the wonder. God is coming .into your life. God is sending a Savior for you to meet every aching need. God is forgiving — forgiving you, even when you find it hardest to forgive yourself.

God is causing the angels in the highest heaven to prepare to sing! And we can hear them preparing all through Advent — most times we don't know exactly what that quiet feeling is, or where the wonder is hiding itself — but I tell you this, God is rooting for us to wake up and seek the wonder, watch for it, as Brugger went in search of the monarchs. Stop. Look. Listen.

Sometimes we are inundated with images of Christmas in Advent. We can become immune to it. Blind, deafened by the din, distracted by the myriad of urgent messages, online, in malls, in our frantic rush to get ready....

But sometimes we catch a glimpse of a tiny image of wonder in Advent. We hear or say "Merry Christmas" or "I love you" so often, but once in a while, the phrase is so full of truth and meaning that our faith is renewed. It could be a carol we hear, or one we are humming to ourselves as we prepare, that transport us. One such carol may be one you know by heart, or one you have to think about, like "I wonder as I wander..." Images of glory: angels, stars, a crèche in a store window that speaks God's truth. They can be overlooked, or they can be amazing.

God is calling us, in our best Advent moments, to wonder. Try it out... delight and disbelief in the same moment. You are free and forgiven. What does it feel like? Will it make a difference in your life? This Advent, say yes....

Come Lord. Fill us up with wonder and with a quiet confidence in God. We wonder, we think, and sometimes we have our doubts. Renew us with the good news that you are indeed coming; through Jesus Christ your Son, our Lord who lives and rules with you and the Holy Spirit, one God, within our world today. Amen.

"Here Am I..."

Luke 1: 26-38. *"In the sixth month the angel Gabriel was sent by God to a town in Galilee called Nazareth, to a virgin engaged to a man whose name was Joseph, of the house of David. The virgin's name was Mary. And he came to her and said, "Greetings, favored one! The Lord is with you." But she was much perplexed by his words and pondered what sort of greeting this might be. The angel said to her, "Do not be afraid, Mary, for you have found favor with God. And now, you will conceive in your womb and bear a son, and you will name him Jesus. He will be great and will be called the Son of the Most High and the Lord God will give him the throne of his ancestor David. He will reign over the house of Jacob forever, and of his kingdom there will be no end." Mary said to the angel, "How can this be, since I am a virgin?" The angel said to her, "The Holy Spirit will come upon you, and the power of the Most High will overshadow you; therefore, the child to be born will be holy; he will be called Son of God. And now, your relative Elizabeth in her old age has also conceived a son; and this is the sixth month for her who was said to be barren. For nothing will be impossible with God. Then Mary said, "Here am I, the servant of the Lord; let it be with me according to your word." Then the angel departed from her."*

This is, of course, is the classic text of the annunciation to Mary, and in the phrases of Luke's story, this is the way by which many of us first begin to focus on the coming of Jesus Christ. My wife, Ruth, told me about an extraordinary Advent experience she had just a few years ago. Not quite as extraordinary as Mary or Elizabeth's Advent wonders, but moving nonetheless. I wrote her story down in a journal, and reread it recently: It was late Advent, and as she was walking down the corridor at our Saint Matthew Church, the winter sunlight was shining extravagantly in through the glass doorway ahead of her, as she looked out into the parking lot on her way to her next errand. The Christmas wreaths were hanging there, and they focused her vision, even from the rear, as she looked out through the clear glass doors through the centers of those evergreen circles. She was seeing through that focused line of sight, looking toward Christmas, and the circle of the wreath was framing all she saw, as well as all that she remembered! She said it made her smile, and hearing it, I smiled too and I wrote it down.

Ruth's mind was looking through the circle of the wreath from behind, and many of her past Christmases were in her mind… the Christmas of Ryan's first two-wheeler, the year we spent in the ER, with Ruth getting stitches in her palm from a broken serving plate while the crowd of the extended family enjoyed Christmas dinner at our home with Ryan as maître d'! The year of her favorite Christmas sermon that I preached, the rides to and from Christmas Eve worship that she and Ryan took all through his childhood, looking at the wonder while counting the houses decorated with Christmas lights, and often enjoying the splendor of the moon reflecting on the snow or shining through the naked trees as they drove to church or back home again that holy night.

May it be like that for each of us in these closing days of Advent; may the things we see and hear and say and do be done within the focused framework of this holy time of expectation and announcement. Gabriel notwithstanding, may God open our hearts to the possibility of sharing Mary's embrace of the joy to come. "Here am I…". Whether the rustle of an angel's wings gets our attention, or the eternal evergreen circle of God's promise of a Savior, festively adorned by red bows (or in Advent blue, as they were at Saint Matthew), whatever the thing is that catches us unawares; whatever it is, may you know your journey is in its last phase. The fourth candle is lit, the days are dwindling down until we have the joy and the smiles of Christmas blessings — the abundance of what's next!

Another journal entry, from another Advent, tells of Ruth and I driving together to get to somewhere important, during another fourth week of Advent. In the car, going about our own busy flurry of preparations, we heard a young Irish woman singing "O Little Town of Bethlehem" on the local college radio station. It was lovely; her voice was light and pure, but it was the wrong tune! We both recognized the melody from another carol we could not place, yet the more we struggled to figure it out, the more we began to realize how much we loved what we were listening to. Not as a replacement, but a renewal.

The joy of Christmas is eternal, like a circle; there is no real beginning and no real ending, there is always renewal and right now, Christmas is very near too. Like the circle of the wreath, the focus is on the promise that renews itself each and every year. We are told that Jesus Christ, the Son of God, will enter our human story; and even as we retell the story each year, even though we well know that "No ear may hear his coming, but in this world of sin, where meek souls will receive him still, the dear Christ enters in…" So, with a quiet confidence, we dip ourselves again into the richness of the promise: "He will be great, and will be called the Son of the Most High, and the Lord God will give to him the throne of his ancestor David. He will reign over the house of Jacob forever, and of his kingdom there will be no end." No end. — Advent is just the beginning.

May this particular week of Advent become a time for you to create special memories. And may the coming of Christmas this year also be deeply enriched by the splendid focus and renewal of remembrances of all your Christmases. Christmas is one of those magical times when you can dip yourself into every Christmas you have ever known. They will just wash over you if you let them. If only you can just remember to say, or pray, or hope: "Here am I…" May we all squint, just a little, to peer through some Christmas wreath, or some prism of your own making; may you find an insight known, or seen, or heard, only by you. One, that if not written down, will still, always, be remembered….

Dear God, we are joyous at the news. A child will be born. We too are rushing about in preparation for his coming. May our preparation find a quiet focus and a joyous fulfillment as he comes among us this year. Because, after all — here we are. Amen.

Those Days / These Days

Luke 2:16-17 *"So they went with haste and found Mary and Joseph, and the child lying in the manger. When they saw this, they made known what had been told them about this child."*

Make no mistake about it, Luke gave us a solemn beginning. "In those days," he said… "when the decree went out from Caesar Augustus, when Quirinius was Governor in Syria… when Mary and Joseph went to be registered… because there was no place for them in the inn…"

"Those days" were a key beginning of course, we know the events of those days, we have been remembering them together all through these weeks of Advent. We recount them every year at this time. Luke was intentional in telling us about "those days" and wanted us to remember how powerful the emperor was, calling people from the whole Roman world to get up and get going.

Luke also meant to show us the exhausting, loving struggle of Mary and Joseph in these days, drawing near, finally, to Bethlehem, so that we would remember it well and so we would also remember that after the struggle of the journey, "The time came for her to be delivered… and she wrapped him in bands of cloth and laid him in a manger." Remember? Of course you do… You remember well what happened in "those days." Caesar's proclamation got the ball rolling; people got up and got going, just as you have been doing all these Advent days.

Then the scene shifts away from the manger in the dimly lit cave that served as a stable behind the inn; we are transported by the story just outside of town, to the night's deep darkness blanketing a hillside in Judea, where those hard-working, scruffy, wipe-your-feet-before-you-come-in shepherds saw their darkness split and lit by God's light. "In those days."

An angel of the Lord spoke, and then a multitude of the heavenly host — a myriad of angels, a crowd of singers — sang. "Glory to God in the highest heaven," that's where we've been, that's what we do there, we praise God, and now we're doing it here on this hillside: "Glory to

But Mary Kept All These Things

God in the highest heaven, and peace to God's people on earth."

It was not the Pax Romana of Caesar's peace, not any earthly ruler's peace... "My peace I give to you, not as the world gives... do not let your hearts be troubled...". This is nothing other than God's lasting peace being set within you. God's peace for your soul, God's peace in your anxious broken places, God's peace and healing throughout your whole life and for the lives of those you cherish. From way up there, to way down here. Heaven's light, peace and healing wholeness came down to earth on that dark hillside in those days, but not in "those days" only.

We know what the angel of the Lord said as he articulated the promise of God. What did the shepherds do on hearing of such a boon? "They went with haste and found Mary and Joseph, and the child lying in a manger...". They saw the scene of peace. "For to you is born this day...", 'unto us is born...' The shepherds quoted the angel of the Lord, who quoted Isaiah even as Handel quoted the angel of the Lord... "Unto us a child is born, unto us a son is given... and he shall be called Wonderful Counselor, Mighty God, Everlasting Father, Prince of Peace." Quite a list of names for a baby.

"For to you is born..." But notice how the time signature changes, from "in those days" — to "this day." It is so close now. "For to you is born 'this day' in the city of David a Savior, who is Christ the Lord." And the shepherds left "with haste" to see for themselves. A Savior, Christ, the Lord, which is what we shall call him. His name is Jesus, and he will save his people from their sins. This day, this will be a sign for you; this day, you will find a babe wrapped in swaddling clothes, and lying in a manger. This day — a Savior, Christ, the Lord. This day — this day, this night, we are so close to gathering to sing, with those angels; to listen, with those scruffy shepherds; to remember the story of what happened "in those days."

This day, in the darkness that sometimes blankets our lives, we light our four Advent candles, to say that we are yearning this day to believe that the story and the promise of those days will still be true this day. We are yearning to believe that our God is sending a Savior. Christ the Lord is coming to us to bring peace and hope, comfort and joy, healing, justice and mercy, forgiveness and favor, remembrance and hope. It is coming to you — so soon now.

You can see the holy family now, in your mind's eye. You can see the shepherds hastening to the stable. Now see them all, surrounded by you and yours — the holy family and your family, those scruffy

71

shepherds and your scruffy acquaintances.

As you light the fourth candle, see the light of Christ, the Savior, Christ, the Lord. Yearn to follow his gentle, yet urgent way in response to God's plan for your healing and your wholeness. Make your way to the place in your life, the place in your heart, soul, mind, and memory, where God is present, active, and loving. The place where it is, has been, and always will be true; that you believe with a quiet confidence that you have a Savior, Christ, the Lord; the babe in the manger, the man on the cross, the Savior striding forth form the empty tomb — toward you. For to you will be born a Savior, Christ, the Lord. I can hardly wait either.

Our Father, we marvel at the amazing promises surrounding your Son. We trust your living word as the bearer of new life and new wholeness for our hastening, hopeful world. We are almost ready to tell others what we shall see and hear, in the power of your Holy Spirit. Strengthen us with your love. Amen.

By Another Road

Matthew 2:12 *"And having been warned in a dream not to return to Herod, they left for their own country by another road."*

Is your tree up yet? Eventually beneath your Christmas tree, there will probably be presents, a village scene, a crèche, or some combination, some assortment of accoutrements placed there on some vestigial schedule (gifts last in my house, after Santa). Or perhaps just a plain simple tree skirt will lie there, gathering needles as they fall from the tree the next two weeks. But no matter what, the tree inside the house is a reminder that the followers of God can transform the ordinary in the service of faith.

What will be on top of your tree? My grandmother had something I still see in a few stores today… it looked like an orb, a ball, but with a tall vertical point, like a spike… I'm not sure what it's called or what it means. There are also tree toppers for sale that celebrate Frosty the Snowman, candy canes, or even the Grinch. Some folks have nothing on top of their tree.

Perhaps you have an angel or a star. They are the symbols of the way people first learned of the gift. Place an angel on top, and you remind everyone that the shepherds will listen to the angels and right away, travel to the town to find the stable and the manger and the holy family. The angel of the Lord is the messenger, the angel on top of the tree is the image of the messenger of God who brought the good news to the shepherds, and to you!

You may have a star atop your tree, as if above the stable, bright in the night sky over Bethlehem. When a friend's daughter was small, she got the part of the Bethlehem star in a Christmas play. After the first rehearsal she came home with her costume, a star shape in shiny gold fabric designed to drape over her like a poncho. "What exactly will you be doing in the play?" Her father asked. "I just stand there and shine," she told him. I've never forgotten that response.

It is that shining star that inspired the magi, the wise ones everywhere, and revealed to them that a new king was born in Bethlehem of Judea. It guided them toward the newborn king. They followed that message of revelation and on Epiphany they arrived in the right place, after asking directions of a conniving and sneaky King Herod. They worshiped the child king, the Wonderful Counselor, the Prince of Peace. It was a culmination of sorts.

What's on top of your tree? What has a messenger told you? God is in the same region as you and me. What got you moving across the Advent wilderness of your life, or was it whom? Was it a parent, a sibling, a teacher, a poem, or a story, a piece of music, Mary's openness to God's will, Joseph's willingness to fall in with God's plan, God's messenger in the heavens, a star, or the exquisite tracery of trees against a winter sky? Was it a childhood memory renewed after a time away? Or were you preparing Christmas for your children this Advent and had your faith renewed… or are you still waiting?

Amazingly, those shepherds and those Magi are never heard from again in scripture. They both exit the scene. It is not that they messed up. It is that God inspired them, invited them to see the gift, to go to approach the gift, to receive it into their lives, and then to return to their lives. You and I are invited to do the same. The shepherds returned glorifying and praising God for all they had heard and seen. Some of us will glorify God soon in song, in prayers, in candlelight, in images of love and celebration, reminded of forgiveness and power and comfort and joy. Then we can head home, glorifying and praising the Lord, as the shepherds did that first time in Bethlehem.

You might try something else too, this year. Go home by another road, as the Magi did, Emulate the Magi, look up to see a star, turn toward it, then double back if you have to, and head where you belong, head home by another road. Yes, simply take another road home, even if it takes a little longer. Turn your back on all the sneaky connivers' episodes in our lives.

Everyone leaves eventually. Everyone but Mary, she stayed and pondered. When your journey is over, whether this Advent, or your Christmas is shaped by the angel who invited the shepherds or the star which guided the Magi, try the magic of my trifecta.

Worship, when the time is right, and then return, having praised God like the shepherds; go home by another road like the Magi. In the days and weeks to come, ponder all these things like Mary did, don't just remember. Converse with them, compare them, throw them side by side and consider the implications, live with these tried and true images of

But Mary Kept All These Things

God's yearning to be present in your life.

Don't come to the child this year expecting a different thing, come to the child expecting to see things differently... By the time you are ready to undecorate your Christmas tree, receive the gift that redeems you, this great joy which is for all the people. Yes, it is for all the people, but it is also for you and yours. So, to return to an early question: what's on top? Whichever it is, angel or star, whatever is on top, wrap it very gently as you carefully lay it to rest till next year....

O God, you have shown yourself to our world, by angel and star. We have almost arrived at our destination. And soon we will find paradoxically, that our journey is not yet over. Continue to guide us, always toward you, from grace to grace. Renew us today with a glimpse of your power. Amen.

The German Shepherd

John 1:14. *"And the word became flesh and dwelt among us, full of grace and truth."*

Years and years ago I began reading the Christmas gospel before the Christmas Eve sermon, with an added twist. When future religious archeologists discover that pulpit Bible, they will see that the Luke 2 text is all marked up, filled with reminders for me... a circle drawn around the word "Joseph," also "Mary," 'the babe lying in a manger, "the shepherds," the "flocks," "the angel of the Lord," the "heavenly host." Because holding the pulpit Bible in the aisle and reading aloud, with the children arrayed up front, each holding a figure from the story that I had provided, I would pause at each circled character. First is Joseph; a child puts him down on the small table there, and one by one other characters, as they are named, (and circled) in the story are placed on the table, then "shepherds," and after the flurry of ten shepherd children, I pause I say out loud for all to hear: "and who has the German Shepherd?" And that child comes to place a German Shepherd dog figure down in front of the manger, and I would say, "the Lutheran presence at the nativity"... and get a laugh.

But here is the most amazing truth — we all want to be there — we all want to believe that we are invited to be there — German Lutherans like me, ladies and gentlemen, boys and girls, children of all ages, of every denomination and ethnicity, whether we are dog owners or just dog lovers. We all want to find ourselves circled in the gospel, so someone will call our name and pause, and we can step forward to pay our respects to the holy child in the manger. Imagine being called into the stable then: the flickering shadows, the smell of the fodder, the hay on the floor, the animals breathing, Joseph holding his lantern with a candle in it so you can peer down into the manger and see the child.

The shepherds' story acknowledges what the church has faithfully taught us for over 2,000 years; your name is circled. I came to know that vividly one summer vacation day as a child.

But Mary Kept All These Things

The small German Shepherd figure I use is made of porcelain. It is two inches long and a bit more than an inch high. It was a gift that came when I thought I was being neglected. Not circled at all. Ever have a day like that? I know, right? One of those "what's in it for me...." days.

Many years ago, I was a very, very happy ten-year-old vacationing at my Aunt Hazel and Uncle Don's farm in Minnesota. One rainy afternoon I spent a day back in town, back in Ruthton, population: 327. My sister was there, at our Grandma Lily's Dress Shop. I was walking through Nancy's domain, seeing all the things she had been doing, hearing her six-year-old voice proudly saying what great fun it was to work at Grandma Lily's shop. "Look and see all the presents I got: a new dress and an apron and this handkerchief with daisies on it." I was completely forgetting the cowboy hat that Uncle Don had bought for me, to keep the sun off my head when we were baling hay, I was feeling a little neglected as I looked down into Nancy's shopping bag full of charming things... "When what to my wondering eyes did appear.." no, that's another story. But Grandma Lily did appear, and took me by the hand and led me to a small double shelf near the back of the store on the right. It held a splendid array of pairs of small porcelain dogs: red Irish setters, beagles, labs, scotties, collies, and poodles. "Pick a pair out for yourself," she said. Delighted, I chose a pair of German Shepherd dogs.

I squirreled them away for years, forgotten mostly, and then miraculously found them without knowing I was looking for them years later, as a new groom, we put them near our new manger scene in our first home. Years after that, I began the quirky Christmas Eve story narrative for the children. Mary and Joseph and the babe lying in a manger, with the shepherds and their flocks, and the angels, and yes, the German Shepherd dog too.

It always got a laugh. But it revealed the honest-to-God sober truth of salvation, the blunt truth of the incarnation, that God so loved the world that he sent his son, from way up there to way down here, "The word became flesh and dwelt among us," It's not a laughing matter at all, is it? But it is joyful.

That is our one true joy, that along with Mary and everyone and the German Shepherd too, the good news of Christ's birth is for you. *For you.* So, whenever you are feeling neglected, you might remember this holy truth: "The word became flesh" for you. The gift of forgiveness is for you, the celebration includes you. Your name is circled.

O God, in the midst of our busy preparations, you are coming.

But Mary Kept All These Things

Mystery surrounds your incarnation, and yet we are filled with joy. Circle us Lord, and bring us the sure and certain hope that responds with grace, joy and thanksgiving. In the name of our coming Lord we pray. Amen.

The Best Christmas "_____" ...
An Advent Adventure

Luke 2:8-9. *"And in that region there were shepherds out in the field, keeping watch over their flock by night. And an angel of the Lord appeared to them, and the glory of the Lord shone around them, and they were filled with fear."*

The Covid Christmas of 2020 seemed a sure bet for "worst" didn't it?

Certainly, on some levels perhaps, the most "filled with fear."

In faith and hope, I tried to recall pieces of other Christmases, and sought out the "bests" that my addled memory cells could dredge up to shine some lights that just might help vanquish the deep shadows of loss, the incomprehensible tragedy of so many deaths, and the sad daily complications of Covid. It was not really a sermon I suppose, but rather some brighter "Glory of the Lord" Christmas remembrances spoken into the darkness of a time that often seemed way too uncertain... way too fearful.

So here goes...

Best Christmas Sweater: A soccer shirt, a gift from my son, Ryan, way back when my beloved Francesco Totti was captain of Roma and helped Italia win the World Cup in... 2006... not ugly at all!

Best Christmas Song: "Christmas in the Trenches" Discovered years and years ago listening to a college radio station during Advent while sitting in a Dunkin' Donuts parking lot. John McCutchen singing live at Wolf Trap. I still have the cassette, and listen every year to the story-song he wrote to recall a moment of peace in the center of WWI one Christmas Eve in France... "'Tis Silent Night' says I, and in two tongues, one song filled up that sky..."

Best Christmas Movie: "Charlie Brown Christmas"- with Linus reciting from Saint Luke ".... And the angel said to them, 'Be not afraid; for behold, I bring you good news of a great joy which will come to all the people; for to you is born this day in the city of David a Savior, who

But Mary Kept All These Things

is Christ the Lord. And this will be a sign for you: you will find a babe wrapped in swaddling clothes and lying in a manger.'... That's what Christmas is all about Charlie Brown." Of course, Honorable Mention has to go to *It's A Wonderful Life*; my wife Ruth had read recently in the NY Times that Jimmy Stewart's tears on the bridge were unscripted... swelling up from his tortured soul after serving in battle in the Second World War — his first movie after returning home... I know Christmases to come will find my eyes damp once or twice as I recall the trials our nation's families faced in the Christmas of 2020. I needed to hear "be not afraid."

Best Christmas Dinner: A flat out tie. Goose, being my idea thirty years ago, and Ruth falling in with my plan for a one-off of newness; and Ruth's most wonderful boeuf bourguignon, her masterpiece for these recent years, creating and sustaining a tradition that still lives on...

Best Piece of Christmas Mail: A letter from my granddaughter Petra a few years ago... I've saved it, and I display it on my desk in Advent, with her envelope addressed to "Grandpa Carter." Inside was her list for Santa. She didn't have his address but she had mine and trusted me to get it to him. It had eleven items, including "Slime, Brooklyn and Bailey merch, a blue collar for Winnie that fits, and a paw print necklace...". It is one of my treasures. Trust — in Advent we are called to trust God.

Best Covid Mask: A gift from Ruth in Advent so I could be ready... it has Christmas trees on it. Yes, even last Christmas had a best... As I think about Mary and Joseph's arduous journey from Nazareth to Bethlehem, the 10:00 am Christmas Eve stocking and gift-delivery trek to our sons family in Easton and back seems almost biblical. We all wore masks, and sat for a few minutes in the cold on their porch and watched eyes glimmer and smile, and heard real voices in the air with no zoom grids to keep centered. A good... mask. Kind of a sad drive home though.

That year in the pandemic, Ruth and I held stockings to be a necessity. Santa left them early at our house, he simply knew that the old way would work. His deliveries were so much more complicated with social distancing and all... so we delivered them that morning surreptitiously to our son and knew that they would find their way to the mantle later and into his and Petra and Caitlin's hands and Winnie's paws right on time Christmas morning in their beautiful new Christmas home.

I suspect it was a long, aching Advent for you and yours last year. It would have been an anxious labor for Mary, her first child and all. It was hard for Joseph too in his uncertainty and their long journey. Up in the close and holy darkness of heaven, where the agony of what was in store for Christ was known, it was anguish. God in Christ inserts himself into the center of our lives, into the close and holy darkness of our prayers. For us and for our salvation, the Son of God came down from heaven. Nothing less is in the manger, the Son of God. Nothing less lies in Joseph's lantern glow. Nothing less than the resurrection and the life. Jesus Christ is the light of the world; the light no darkness can overcome — ever.

Finally, my nominee for Best Christmas Memory: Kneeling in the candlelit grotto in Bethlehem in Palestine in 1992 is a great memory; but in my best moments, I'm still patient and hopeful... Ruth and I believe that "the best is yet to come."

How about you? Give it a try in just a few days. Your answers will be different — you may even use some different categories; but I believe the fun of sorting through names and feelings and catching glimpses of your own heart in the process of remembering them, will bring you joy. I know I've held some fear at bay in writing this — and I've enjoyed that part of my own Advent adventure.

Great and gracious Lord, be with us in the dark moments and lift our eyes to see and enjoy the brightening of the dawn of our salvation, our healing, and our forgiveness; through your Son, Jesus Christ our Lord. Amen.

Save The Bows

Luke 2:10. *"And the angel said to them, 'Be not afraid; for behold, I bring you good news of a great joy which will come to all the people...'"*

When we think of Christmas, most of us think of gifts. When we think of gifts, many of us think back to the joyful ruins of a Christmas Eve or Christmas morning when we were children, piles of paper and ribbon scattered around, beautiful bows tossed aside. For many with younger children and for many who are children, or for those of us who are proudly still children at heart, this scene is not a history lesson, it is soon to be a current event. Perhaps tonight in your family, but the Carters always wait till Christmas Day....

When I was a child, my parents asked my sister Nancy and me to save the large pieces of wrapping paper — fold it carefully for next year's use — save those gift boxes, bows too! Tomorrow morning, my family will save the bows — they are tossed deliberately under the little cherry coffee table in the living room where the tree lives. The tree that grows gifts magically beneath the boughs sometime between Christmas Eve worship and Christmas morning — the bows live in a riot of color under the table. Like children. I don't know why we save the bows. It's like a connection for me to my parents who are gone now, and all those gifts and all those joyful times with happy people. It's a little silly, but I'm glad we save the bows.

The remnant of bows involves recalling what we have given, not just what we got. What we have put together for our family and our friends. In our best moments the searching and careful thought is akin to a spiritual pilgrimage to find the right present for the right person from the right person; a trinity of the right gift for the right person, from the right person. We capture the spirit and the soul of the person and bring alive our relationship. I cannot remember all my presents over the years, but I do remember the people.

This reminds me, and I hope you, that the gift is but a means to define, develop and express the relationship we have. Most days of the year we hold back, most days we do not squander or lavish our affection on people to whom we are devoted. But on Christmas the gift is sometimes a way to say what we often dare not say without it– "I care about you, I'm devoted to you, and I want you to know it." The right gift can speak volumes. "Thank you" we respond, "You shouldn't have" we say, "Oh, it's nothing at all" we reply, but of course it is everything, it says *everything*. It is meant to.

The gift says I love you and I love being loved by you. Christmas Eve is the very image of that, the very image of love. Not to sound heretical, but the child in the manger is not the end or even the object of this holy time. The child in the manger is the means whereby God's love is presented to the people whom God loves. God says, "I love you and I love being loved by you." He gives the gift of a Savior, Jesus Christ.

The birth of Jesus is many, many things. It is a miracle, it is a mystery, it is mercy, it is an antidote to fear, and it is a gift. It is truly, God's gift to God's people. "And the angel said to them, "Be not afraid; for behold, I bring you good news of a great joy which will come to all the people."

Christmas is God reaching out to establish and sustain or, perhaps, restore a relationship with us, with you. It is a relationship of love. It is of this love the child Jesus is the sign and the symbol and the substance. "I love you and I love being loved by you."

The joy is the renewal of love even against all the forces of this dark, cold world. We know about the world. We suspect the world is never going to be perfect. It is never going to be filled with the angels' song of peace on earth, good will to all. This world, we suspect, cannot deliver Christmas as we want it, because this world cannot deliver Christ. You actually know that though, don't you? But Christ does come into our dark, cold world, our world, amidst the many Christmas worlds of museums, malls, Dickens, and Radio City Music Hall. Christmas comes – God deliverers Christ, and Christ is present as the present… the gift of God for the salvation of all — "all the people."

Sometimes we just want Christmas to be a quaint, pure antidote to the real world, eradicating the dark commercialism of a world that has seemingly lost its way. But remember, that the Christmas joy and our need for bows begins with Caesar Augustus and Governor Quirinius, it begins in a dark, cold world, in a real and fallen world, one quite similar to ours. And here in our world, we are attracted not to a mall or a concert or a show, but to this Christ child.

The attraction of the gift of Christ is precisely the fact of our faith that Christ is given to this real world of ours, this world of concerts and shows and malls. This world of homelessness, of injustice and war; a world of broken homes, broken dreams, a world of illness, aging, and dying. This is God's great gift that comes to us in our real world. Into this world the gift comes and it returns us to the joy every single year.

Come he has, and come he will, and come again he will, though we do not deserve it. Since we cannot explain this or even understand it, all we can do is receive the gift and say "Thank you," and "You shouldn't have," and discover that the gift, this gift is not "nothing at all," it is everything. It says "I love you and I love being loved by you."

Some will say it takes male foolishness or a German act of will or an Irish imagination to see all this in the detritus of bows tossed haphazardly under a coffee table in a room with a Christmas tree. But I say it takes courage to receive this gift of joy at Christmas. It takes courage to acknowledge our need. Courage to acknowledge that we are known by God, and that we are loved by God anyway. It takes courage to be the semi-generous, undeserving recipient of such a generous gift. Because, to quote Linus, "that is what Christmas is all about, Charlie Brown." It is God's gift for God's people — the gift of Jesus the Christ. And Jesus said "I love you, and I love being loved by you." Enjoy the gift. Save the bows!

Great God, we are filled this day with so much Christmas Eve joy. We give you thanks for this wonderful gift. A Savior — for us. Thank you Father, for Jesus Christ your Son our Lord, who lives and rules with you and the Holy Spirit, one God, within our world today. Amen.

Faith Rewarded

John 1:1-5: *"In the beginning was the word, and the word was with God, and the word was God. He was in the beginning with God. All things came into being through him, and without him not one thing came into being. What has come into being with him was life, and the life was the light of all people. The light shines in the darkness, and the darkness did not overcome it."*

Merry Christmas! In the twenty-first century, as in every century, there is often a deep, under-the-skin yearning for a spiritual life: meditation, peace, trust, and worship. Christmas is one of the most welcoming doorways into God's presence in the history of the world, wide open to all the past, and revealing God's presence forever and ever, Amen. Christmas is about a new beginning.

Imagine Mary and Jesus in the dark stable, perhaps a lantern held by Joseph, and the shepherds on their dark midnight hillside, stars, perhaps a moon, maybe not, maybe a campfire. We need to get close to the manger, the creche, on a table at home, under the tree, in a painting or on a Christmas card... what for you is the climactic moment in the story? Feelings of devotion are aroused by things seen and things heard, the angels sang on that hillside because of what they had seen and been told in heaven! The message to the shepherds is climaxed with a song.

The shepherds were in awe; their faces reveal that they are almost mesmerized by the angels. In the darkness of their lives they are recipients of the message of the light that will transform their lives. No *almost* about it.

Light filling the darkness is a primary spiritual metaphor of Christmas. Joseph has his lantern, the wise men have their star, the shepherds have the glory of the heavenly host. Jesus Christ is the light of the world. The light no darkness can overcome.

Lost in wonder and excitement, the shepherds' mouths are agape. Neither cynical or exuberant, but mesmerized by the experience. Recall them as they reverently listened to the angels, then spoke to one another, then went to see and speak to the holy family, telling them all they had heard and seen. Their heads were bowed, not gazing at the child directly in a fearful respect that one gives an occurrence outside the realm of usual experience. It was a spiritual experience. Regard them well.

I think they knelt impulsively before the baby, adoring Jesus reverently, mirroring in advance the wise men, who will fall on their knees to honor the child as king, paying him homage. You see in this montage, the beginnings of faith… Ultimately, their eyes and ours are drawn to the face at the center. Step into the story, look closely, and come with the shepherds to experience the light, the event, the birth of the child. He is the light of the world. Imagine the freedom that is ours to become involved in the story of Jesus Christ on this Christmas Day. Hear the message that the faithful are given. The spiritual blessing of the presence of Christ… that is the effect on the shepherds and later the wise men who come and worship, and on us in our own time, in our own dark moments.

The message is that faith is rewarded with a blessing: being saved from the darkness of death itself… a new creation… he is wrapped in swaddling clothes, wrapped in bands of cloth. The same will happen when he is taken down from the cross — wrapped in a linen shroud. He was salvation from death itself. Even that darkness cannot overcome the light of Christ.

The angels praise God and frame the truth of the story. The ox and the ass were there to frame the holy family and stand in for all humanity, witnesses to the holy light glowing in the center. Mary and Joseph are there to frame the holy Child….

The shepherds, you and I arrive at Christmas to have our spiritual lives renewed, our faith reborn in the angels' song, in the shepherds' eyes, in the flicker of starlight as we adore the child in the manger this very day. Perhaps we might even consider the possibility that we would light a candle, and pause….

I believe the shepherds came before the child one at a time. The individual is important to the Lord of life. The individual is the one who is saved by faith in Christ. You are important to Jesus. The Christmas creche comes to life by including the shepherds, because the story comes alive only by having an audience. The light shines into our darkness this very day by including you and me in the fact of our faith: Christ the Savior is born… Merry Christmas!

Lord of power and might, you have come into the world with your brightness. Your light shines clearly, even in the midst of darkness. May we see your light this day by the light of the gift of faith and ourselves become radiant that others may know your life-giving light. Amen.

Printed in the USA
CPSIA information can be obtained
at www.ICGtesting.com
LVHW090326231123
764661LV00003B/317